The Aspiring Advisor

Moritz Dressel

Copyright © Watlanka Press, 2015
All rights reserved

WATLANKA PRESS
The Aspiring Advisor – Strategies and Tools for a Successful Consulting Career
Moritz Dressel

Copyright © 2015 by Moritz Dressel
All Rights Reserved

Copyeditor: HappyMarli (Freelancer.com)
Cover Design: Sherwin Soy (99designs.com)
Interior Design: Moritz Dressel

All rights reserved. This book was published by the author, Moritz Dressel, under Watlanka Press. No part of this book may be reproduced in any form by any means without the express permission of the author. This includes reprints, excerpts, photocopying, recording, or any future means of reproducing text.

If you would like to do any of the above, please seek permission first by contacting the author at Aspiringadvisor.com.

Printed by CreateSpace, Charleston SC

ISBN 978-1514620717

FREE BONUS ITEMS

Free companion items to this book, including checklists, email templates, printable versions of all graphics and tables, and more, are available at:

AspiringAdvisor.com/bonus

Please access these resources now before you forget.

Note: Due to continuous advancements in how we work as consultants, this book is updated as often as necessary. This is the first version of *The Aspiring Advisor*.

To see what has changed or been added since this version was printed, visit AspiringAdvisor.com/updates.

About the Author

Moritz Dressel is the author of *The Aspiring Advisor.* He is also a management consultant specializing in post-merger integration, joint ventures, and strategic alliances. As a member of a leading M&A practice, he has supported major transformations in various industries, such as manufacturing, life sciences, and energy and utilities.

Moritz Dressel holds a BSc in Public Administration from the University of Twente (NL) and an MSc in Management from the University of Lugano (CH). He can be reached directly via Twitter @MoritzDressel or at moritzdressel.com.

Contents

Part 1: Before You Start 1
    Chapter 1: What You Can Expect 3
    Chapter 2: Getting Ready for Day 1 13

Part 2: When You Start 27
    Chapter 3: How to Survive Your First Week 29
    Chapter 4: You and the Firm 39
    Chapter 5: How to Deliver Great Work 53
    Chapter 6: How to Master Communication by Email 85
    Chapter 7: How to Master Communication by Phone 111
    Chapter 8: How to Manage Meetings Effectively 127
    Chapter 9: How to Manage Your Time 141
    Chapter 10: How to Stay Ahead 153
    Chapter 11: How to Build Your Network 169
    Chapter 12: Using Downtime to Your Advantage 193
    Chapter 13: How to Get Measured Well 199

Part 3: Just Between Us..215
Chapter 14: How to Manage Your Private Life 217
Chapter 15: How to Cover Your Ass 225
Chapter 16: Saying No Without Ruining Your Career 235
Chapter 17: Stop Thinking and Execute 245

Part 4: Leaving the Firm..251
Chapter 18: Should You Leave the Firm?............................253
Chapter 19: If You Decide to Leave the Firm......................257

Final Thoughts..265

Appendix..267

Notes...272

Preface

"Teflon." "You better get it in writing." "Don't forget the most important client." What would *you* make of all that? I didn't always see the relevance right away but soon came to understand that I had better listen. Advice from more experienced colleagues was essential in getting my career started.

Over the following years, my colleagues and I continued to pass on our pieces of wisdom whenever a cool new kid joined the team. Unfortunately, we could not simply hand over a 200-page document and tell him or her to come back if he or she had any questions. That type of manual didn't exist!

At some point, I became frustrated with this state of affairs, so I started to dig a little deeper. I was certain that someone from our industry must have written out what I was looking for. However, that was not the case. I came across a number of resources that looked promising, but in the end, they turned out to be too high-level, lacked specific actions to take, were too industry-agnostic, or were simply not applicable for junior consultants. I needed something more specific. I was looking for a comprehensive guide that I'd never had – a handbook answering all the questions that a junior consultant might have when starting his or her career. Since I was unable to find that resource, this book is intended to fill that gap.

My colleagues and I have noticed that there are common themes with which many junior consultants struggle. By addressing these topics in detail, I hope to provide a comprehensive manual, one that we would have liked to have when we first started out.

Everything in this book is based on my own experience in consulting and the invaluable advice passed on to me. Therefore, the point of view is inherently subjective. However, by incorporating input from other senior and junior practitioners, both in my firm and from competing firms, I believe that the overall picture I present is sound. Any junior consultant should be able to immediately apply the concepts herein.

Who Should Read This Book?

I have written this book with aspiring consultants in mind. What would I have liked to know? What were the questions I asked my senior colleagues? Which questions were repeatedly raised by new hires?

I believe that everyone just starting out in consulting should flip through these pages. However, those who have already gained some experience and are looking for additional tips and tricks will likely find such content in here as well. While this book is specifically targeted at junior practitioners, more senior individuals in the consulting field who have joined from other industries may also benefit.

What Is Covered?

This book begins at the point in the process where an aspiring practitioner has signed his or her work contract. From well before the first day of work up to a potential resignation, common pitfalls and practical remedies are discussed in detail.

It is equally important to clarify what is not included in this book. Material concerning how to find a job in consulting is not included. You will not find advice on how to successfully apply for a job, become a master of case studies, or pass job interviews. This sort of information exists already, and I was not trying to reinvent the wheel.

Likewise, this is not a book explaining how to sell to, manage, and deliver to *external* clients. Navigating the client environment, while important, is not the first order of the day for those starting out at a junior level. We will focus primarily on how to succeed internally, as that is often the starting point for a promising career.

Who Is This Guy?

I am working as a management consultant at one of the leading global consulting practices in Switzerland. I have worked on international engagements serving clients from various industries with colleagues from across a broad network of member firms as well as competitors.

After about four years with the firm, I chose to take some time off to travel through Asia. While on the road, I decided to finally get around to writing the book that I would have personally liked to read when I started my career. I am grateful for the advice I received, but there are a number of lessons learned the hard way that I could have done without. This is what started my work on this book in late October 2014.

While writing this book, I have had my fair share of coffee in Wi-Fi-enabled cafés from bustling Tokyo and Phnom Penh to the islands of Okinawa. I hope that every cup consumed in that process will have been worth it for future consultant generations to come.

Okinawa, Japan, April 2015

How to Read This Book

This book is structured along a consultant "life cycle." Each of the four main parts is composed of different chapters focusing on a specific stage in a junior consultant's career.

Part 1, "Before You Start," focuses on job entry preparation. It sets realistic expectations and details how to have a positive impact from the moment you enter the firm.

Part 2, "When You Start," is all about getting things done. It provides useful tools, teaches vital consulting skills, introduces key people, and lays out strategies to work the system in your favor.

Part 3, "Just Between Us," is a more personal take on a variety of topics. It explains how to manage your private life, protect yourself from getting screwed by others, push back effectively, and find your sweet spot within the organization.

Part 4, "Leaving the Firm," acknowledges the fact that not everyone remains in consulting for their entire professional life. As such, this part provides a career change decision-making framework, as well as specific action steps to take when you are about to leave your consulting firm.

Getting the most out of this book is somewhat dependent on your background. There is a major difference between just starting out in the industry and already having consulting experience. Hence, I suggest that you proceed as follows.

If You Are Just Starting Out

In case you have just secured your first job at a consulting firm, or have an interest in being employed in the industry, I would recommend that you read this book cover to cover at least once. In doing so, you will gain an in-depth understanding of what consulting is all about from an internal perspective and how you can succeed in the industry when just starting out. You can then go back to specific sections that have triggered your interest or that appear particularly relevant for your specific situation.

If You Already Have Some Experience

If you already have a few months (or years) of experience working as a consultant under your belt, you're probably seeking some additional insights that you simply may have missed. Given that, reading this book cover to cover might not be the most efficient approach. Instead, I would suggest that you quickly skim through the book to get an overall understanding of the content by reading the key chapter takeaways and then proceed by reviewing specific sections of interest to you.

Project Example in This Book

Throughout this book, we will make reference to a fictive project example, which makes the concepts more tangible. We will illustrate certain concepts using realistic names and project roles, rather than blank templates.

In the example, called Project "Bantiger,"[1] Pharma Technology Inc. (PTI), a global pharmaceutical company, has asked Consulting Inc. to help improve its sales force effectiveness. To do so, Consulting Inc. will set up a small project team to analyze sales information across Europe and identify potential optimizations.

The following stakeholders will be part of the scenario.

Consulting Inc.

- Adam Mills (Junior Consultant): Adam is our main character. He joined Consulting Inc. one year ago. You should associate with him, i.e., when you read "Adam," you may replace it with your name.

- Henk de Groot (Partner): Henk is Adam's boss and leads a team of consultants. He is glad that Adam was selected to work with PTI for the next six weeks.

- John Wood (Project/Engagement Partner): John is another partner from Consulting Inc. He has worked with PTI many times before and has very close client relationships, particularly with Rupert Brown, PTI's Head of Europe.

- Daniela Lopez (Project Manager): Daniela is an experienced senior manager with Consulting Inc. and serves as Project Manager on the Bantiger project. She will therefore manage Adam on a day-to-day basis.

Pharma Technology Inc.

- Christian Cho (Global CEO): Christian has been with PTI throughout his career and was recently appointed global CEO. One of his first objectives is to enhance the company's profitability. Among other factors, he believes that European sales force effectiveness is lacking in comparison to other regions.

- Rupert Brown (Project Sponsor & Head of Europe): Rupert has been with PTI for more than twenty years and leads the European market. Christian has asked Rupert to make Europe more profitable and wants him to deliver results quickly.

- Jacques Moreau (Project Lead): Jacques leads PTI's Special Projects division. He joined PTI two years ago from another consulting firm and will work closely with the Consulting Inc. project team.

- Philipp Seagull (Finance Analyst): Philipp is part of the Finance team. He will work closely with Consulting Inc., particularly with Adam. He will primarily provide sales figures and clarify any uncertainties.

PTI's headquarters are in Chicago, Illinois. The project team, however, will work from PTI's European headquarters in Amsterdam, the Netherlands.

The project (see Figure 1: Project Bantiger Project Plan) is scheduled to last for six weeks, starting on August 3, 2015. By the end of Week 3, the project team is expected to provide some initial findings of their analysis. The results will be discussed in a Steering Committee Meeting (STC) composed of both parties, including senior leadership.

You do not have to memorize this information. I will provide all the necessary background information when referencing this project example. However, you might want to bookmark this page for easy reference.

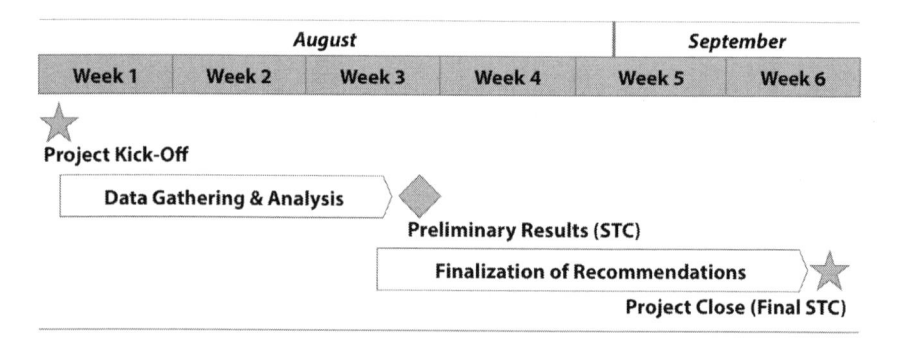

August				September	
Week 1	Week 2	Week 3	Week 4	Week 5	Week 6

★ Project Kick-Off

Data Gathering & Analysis

Preliminary Results (STC)

Finalization of Recommendations

Project Close (Final STC)

Figure 1: Project Bantiger Project Plan

Acknowledgements

Many people have played a role in what ultimately led to publishing this book. There are too many to name here, but the shortlist is as follows.

This book, and the experience that underpins it, would not have been possible without the support of Massimo Garbuio and Frank Herrmann. In fact, my career would have probably turned out very differently without you. Thank you!

Massimo, with respect to this book, your help in getting the initial structure right was absolutely priceless. Once we had a plan for the book in place, I could essentially go on autopilot in October 2014.

Frank, you continued to challenge my thinking and provided invaluable direct feedback (as always!), which made this piece much sharper than I could have ever accomplished alone.

Special thanks to Philipp Schumann; I'm not sure I would have even considered writing a book if it had not been for our discussions during your annual visits to Berlin.

Thank you to everyone who read a draft and provided feedback, especially Florian Welter, Constantin Ulmer, Moritz Mark, and

Benjamin Schumann. Also, thanks to those who didn't read a draft, but tolerated my many rants about getting this over the finish line.

I also want to thank my fellow colleagues and clients. This book is informed by the many hours we have worked together and the lessons I have learnt in that process. I must also mention Christian Shawa, a great teacher, in particular – Thank you!

Finally, I wish to express my deepest gratitude to my parents, Monika and Joachim, for their unconditional love, patience and support throughout those years, and for providing me with all the opportunities in life that a child could ever wish for.

Part 1

Before You Start

PART 1 ESTABLISHES THE BASELINE for the rest of this book. As such, it focuses on the preparation for your job entry. Chapter 1 helps to set the right expectations. Here, we try to shed light on the reality of consulting and destroy some of the most popular myths. Chapter 2 is all about Day 1 readiness. It lays the foundation for having a positive impact from the very first moment you enter the firm.

CHAPTER 1

What You Can Expect

"Reality is frequently inaccurate."

Douglas Adams,
The Restaurant at the End of the Universe

People have shared plenty of stories and anecdotes from the inside of the consulting industry in the past. However, much of that is exaggerated and nowhere close to what most practitioners have experienced. This chapter will set a few things straight and help you start from a more realistic perspective. At the very least, it will save you from joining the circus with complete naiveté.

First, I will address a few popular misconceptions regarding how consulting works and your new colleagues. We will then focus on two aspects that often surprise newcomers, namely the role of "perfection" and the interaction between different hierarchical levels. Finally, we will conclude this chapter on a more positive note regarding the consulting industry.

How Consulting Works

Consultancies are not charities. Just like any other business, they need to return a profit to be sustainable. To accomplish this, their leaders need to strike a fine balance between the resources needed to build a practice and running a profitable business, because ideally, consultants should not sit idle.

When a consultant is not on a project, no revenue is being generated. It does not matter what other activities are being performed instead. Not billing hours to clients is the same as losing money from the firm's perspective. Therefore, it is of paramount importance to have a constantly filled pipeline of projects and upcoming opportunities to reduce or avoid downtime between projects. To accomplish that, certain workflows may have to run in parallel. Consultants who are staffed on a project might occasionally be asked to offer support on proposal work, i.e., preparing pitches to potential clients.

Furthermore, due to the necessity of keeping people staffed, there is not much time for sensitivities either. Some people may find themselves working on projects that are not their greatest desire. Clearly, not all projects, clients, or industries are equal. You simply have to suck it up sometimes. For junior consultants who have long-term goals in the field, there is no real alternative but to take everything as a learning experience and give their best effort. Arguing or complaining won't help. If anything, it will make you look bad and will hurt you in the long run.

Your Colleagues

Now, let's discuss the most important asset of a consulting practice: its people. Again and again, people have asked me what it's like to work in consulting and whether it really was as elite as so many perceive it to be.

An Elitist Circle?

The "elite" are typically defined as a select group of people that stand out by virtue of certain qualities, such as ancestry, wealth, experience, or training. In part, consultants may qualify to be labeled as elite, because practitioners have almost all undergone substantial training and developed a deeper level of expertise in problem-solving, understanding processes, and reading organizations than most people in other career paths. Some would argue that the level of experience across different work settings is also usually higher than in other professions.

There are also those individuals who are unfamiliar with the industry and have a rather negative view on consulting practitioners in general, thereby reinforcing this elitist notion. Frankly, not all of the criticism is unfounded. There are those practitioners who deliver poor value for high rates. However, each transactional relationship involves at least two parties – a service provider and a client.

I strongly believe that the vast majority of practitioners sincerely strive to bring exceptional value to their clients. A lot of people starting out in consulting are attracted by and expect to join this very type of elitist circle. At the minimum, many hold the belief that their future coworkers are top-notch and are generally people from whom to learn. I also started with the expectation that I would soon become part of some inner circle of wisdom, expertise, and never-ending drive for success.

What Is It Actually Like?

It probably comes as no surprise that the truth lies somewhere in between. There is no "standard" consulting practitioner. People differ, just like in every other industry. When you start your new role, you will meet people from all walks of life. Apart from the obvious differences, such as age and personality, your colleagues will also differ in the following three aspects.

- **Education:** Just because many of your classmates wanted to find a job in consulting does not mean that all practitioners have similar educational backgrounds. In fact, nothing could be further from the truth.

Coming up with novel solutions to problems faced by clients requires a broad spectrum of perspectives. This can hardly be achieved when everyone is equipped with the same business degree. Fresh and novel perspectives require different viewing angles of the starting point. Throw some cross-pollination of ideas at the scene and you will see why a multifaceted workforce is key in consulting.

- **Professional background:** In the beginning, the people you work with will likely have a similar background to yourself. They might have just started out, or at most, have a year or so of experience.

When it comes to more senior practitioners, however, you will realize that there are people with all types of professional backgrounds. Some senior figures might have started out just like you and worked their way up the consulting ladder, but there will be plenty of others who have only joined the firm at a later stage in their careers. These include both practitioners joining from competitors and those joining from entirely different industries, often known as industry experts.

- **Motivation:** People have different priorities based on their background and experience. You will meet some practitioners who give their utmost at all times. Serving clients in a challenging work environment with ever-changing requirements is what gets them up in the morning.

However, they are the exception. You will find just as many practitioners who regard the industry merely as any other job, perhaps one that lands them a position at some client company years down the road.

Finally, there are those who tried something else before, did not succeed for one reason or another, and came back to consulting.

You could write an entire book about the aspects that differentiate people in consulting. For now, this is meant to provide a flavor of the different characteristics of the people you will meet and work with. This should have also made it clear that there is no such thing as a "typical consultant." Consultants come from all walks of life, and, in contrast to popular belief, the elite notion might not be overly appropriate.

Let's look at two organizational aspects that are frequent sources of disillusionment for juniors – perfection and interaction between different hierarchical levels.

Perfection Does Not Exist

If you've never worked in the corporate world before, you will be surprised to see what the working reality is actually like. Sometimes, you begin to wonder how some companies can successfully operate, let alone generate a profit. This applies to small companies and Fortune 500 companies alike.

Surprisingly, many consulting firms have significant room for improvement, too. Although this may seem hard to believe, advising clients on best-in-class technology and processes does not require a consulting firm to use equally advanced systems. In other words, many practitioners help implement better stuff than they personally use. Examples are manifold. Let's look at two that you will likely notice yourself.

1. **Technology:** Given the importance of acting quickly to client requests and dynamic market conditions, you would expect all consulting firms to take advantage of the latest technologies. After all, what enables us privately in ways previously unimagined should also be useful in business. The type of work conducted in this industry, however, requires a certain degree of precaution. Risk management is of the utmost importance.

   Therefore, you should quickly come to accept that your privately used devices are probably miles ahead of what you will be using in your daily job. In other words, you may have a Ferrari at home but a horse carriage at the office. There is no need to complain about these specific challenges to your peers. Everyone knows.

   Depending on your firm, the exact shortcomings may differ, but rest assured, you will be disappointed if you expect perfection in terms of:
   - Intuitive and fully functioning enterprise resource planning systems
   - A powerful knowledge-sharing platform
   - Integrated learning platforms (e.g., training calendar per grade, results automatically captured in a performance management system)
   - Accurate client relationship management tools

2. **Internal Processes:** Throughout the industry, processes are not always as clear-cut and straightforward as one would expect. Don't be surprised if you experience lengthy, nontransparent decision-making

processes firsthand or realize that you don't have access rights to the reporting system requiring you to authorize certain payments due to being assigned to a different legal entity in the IT system . . . you get the picture.

To be fair, this complexity is not always the case, but considering that, as an industry, we advise clients on how to implement best practices, our own inefficiencies seem strange.

Interaction between Levels

Now, let's consider the interaction between different hierarchical levels. While not exclusive to consulting, one cannot fail to recognize the hierarchical mindset with which some practitioners enter the career game. What do I mean by hierarchical mindset? The relationship between senior and junior practitioners.

The most common issue is related to the delegation of work. For example, at some point, you will end up working for people who will delegate either a) everything or b) only those tasks that would be commonly called "shitty jobs." Fortunately, you will learn something from every task you undertake at the start of your career.

This becomes more problematic once you have performed certain tasks many times over, and you realize that the only reason you're asked to do it again is because your senior figure is a) too lazy or b) does not have a clue how to do it himself or herself. These moments are painful, and we have all gone through them.[2] (For specific guidance on this, please refer to Chapter 16.)

Similarly, some senior individuals, regardless of their level, are happy to forget the team spirit when it comes to their own private matters. Don't get me wrong; there should be a life outside work. But leaving with a hypocritical, *"But don't stay too long,"* while expecting juniors to work all night is just wrong.

Both of these examples are just that – examples. There are many other situations in which you can experience the hierarchical food chain in practice. The problem is, most juniors get so fed up that by the time they are in a senior position, they consider it perfectly normal to engage in the same behavior. Don't let that happen to you. Apart from those "senior exploits junior" anecdotes, you will likely be in awe once you see your hellish manager cowering in front of his boss. Many senior colleagues will become so fixated on their next promotion that it becomes hard for them to speak up. Even if they have a point, you will rarely see seniors correct their boss. It does happen but not often enough.

On the positive side, those who do speak their mind are usually widely recognized and respected. This is not because they speak up to their boss, per se, but because they usually hold themselves to a higher standard in everything that they do. Making one's position known when it serves the greater good is just one facet of their attitude to work. They are led by principle and they lead by example.

In a nutshell, you will meet people with different backgrounds and different mindsets. There will also be people you will quickly learn to avoid. However, there will be plenty of others who will happily have you on their team and will support you in your development. Suck it up when you interact with the former, and start seeking out the latter.

On the Bright Side

Let's close this chapter on a more positive note. Despite what I've touched upon so far, you should look forward to working in consulting. I am of the firm opinion that this is the best platform to start one's professional career.[3] I am not aware of any other industry that provides such an outstanding learning environment. If you are, please let me know.

Do you want a steep learning curve from Day 1? Do you want to change clients often, allowing you to quickly gain insights into numerous different organizations and corporate cultures? Are you hungry for different projects that challenge even the most experienced professionals because no client engagement is ever the same? If you answered yes to those questions, then you are in the right place! Clearly, it will not always be easy. You will run into obstacles, but you will also learn from them. You will meet resistance and unfair treatment, but you are more than capable of growing through it.

Key Takeaways

- Roll up your sleeves. Consulting is not a charity. Help keep the firm running, whether through supporting a project or making proposals – or both.

- Be open to working in a diverse organization. Your colleagues come from all walks of life, and you might not have anything in common besides handing out the same business card.

- Don't set your hopes too high as consulting firms are not the epitome of perfection. Whether related to technology or internal processes, expect to find plenty of room for improvement.

- Stay close to true leaders. Don't get bogged down by hierarchical games; instead, identify and connect with those who lead not by virtue of rank but by example.

- Expect setbacks as in any other industry, but be confident in the knowledge that consulting provides one of the most rewarding career starts through a steep and constant learning curve from Day 1.

CHAPTER 2
Getting Ready for Day 1

> *"By failing to prepare, you are preparing to fail."*
>
> **Benjamin Franklin**

FIRST IMPRESSIONS MATTER. At a time where apps like Tinder flourish, few would argue that appearance is unimportant at first sight. This chapter attempts to set you on the right track by illustrating how to lay the groundwork for a successful career.

To a large degree, it is when people meet for the first time that opinions about one another are made. In fact, the initial meeting is often the very beginning of the relationship that determines its future. Whether you will "click" with your colleagues is largely dependent on how they perceive you upon first being introduced to you. This is what we will delve into in this chapter.

First, I will emphasize the importance of Day 1 readiness and why so many people fail. We will then look more closely at what Day 1 readiness means for you and how to achieve it.

Why Day 1 Readiness?

Day 1 readiness is a classic business term that is commonly used in large-scale implementation or transformation projects. It is defined as the minimum criteria to be met in order to pass a key milestone in a project plan. What every project team is working toward is the day when a new "reality" sets in (e.g., a new IT system goes live or a legal separation is completed).

Why does this matter to you? In a way, you need to prepare yourself for your own Day 1. It is your first day in consulting and most likely your first day at work. You are joining a world full of ambition and the constant demand for excellence. To facilitate a smooth transition into this new world, you will want to set yourself up for success.

What Most People Get Wrong

Most new joiners could get much more out of their experience in consulting. What got them into the job is actually quite close to what will also get them ahead. When applying, most people invest an enormous amount of time preparing for job interviews, assessment centers, brainteasers, etc. Landing the job usually takes time, but practice does eventually make perfect.

Once the contract has been signed, however, most people go back on autopilot. Celebrating your first steps in your dream industry is great but starting without special preparation is not. Don't get me wrong, celebrations and quality time have their place, but I believe that everyone should at least squeeze in an hour or two thinking through what needs to happen for a successful first day at work.

I hope that the previous two sections drove home the importance of systematically preparing for your own Day 1.

Objectives for Your Day 1

Put yourself in the shoes of your future colleagues for a moment. What kind of person would you like to have on your team or project? Which character traits would you value most? Also, what would turn you off or earn the new joiner a spot on your mental blacklist (i.e., you would not consider him or her for projects)? If you were to ask my colleagues and me, we would tell you something like the following.

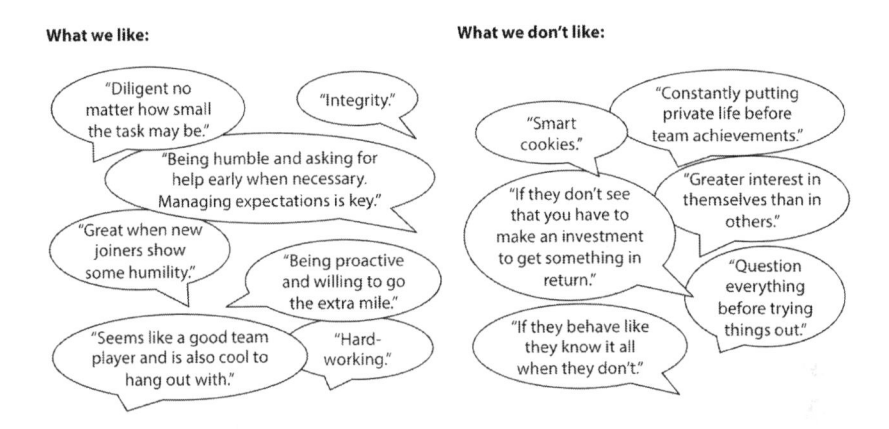

What we like:
- "Diligent no matter how small the task may be."
- "Integrity."
- "Being humble and asking for help early when necessary. Managing expectations is key."
- "Great when new joiners show some humility."
- "Being proactive and willing to go the extra mile."
- "Seems like a good team player and is also cool to hang out with."
- "Hard-working."

What we don't like:
- "Smart cookies."
- "Constantly putting private life before team achievements."
- "If they don't see that you have to make an investment to get something in return."
- "Greater interest in themselves than in others."
- "Question everything before trying things out."
- "If they behave like they know it all when they don't."

From this, we can derive a specific set of objectives that you should consider taking to heart (Table 1: Day 1 Objectives). Remember that people are often short on time, so they have to form an opinion quickly. Hence, the closer you can be to meeting these objectives by coming across accordingly, the brighter your future in the firm is likely to be.

Objective	You want to come across as being…
Likeability	Humble, modest, sociable, essentially a "nice guy," conveying an interest in other people
Drive	A self-starter, looking for ways to accomplish things, helpful to the team, proactively asking how to support best
Motivation	Interested in the work of other people, willing to work hard, conveying a sense of pride to be part of the firm
Client readiness	Reliable, trustworthy, professional, sharp, knowing your role (junior vs. senior, service provider vs. client)

Table 1: Day 1 Objectives

What to Prepare for Day 1 and How

There are a million ways that someone starting out in a new job can prepare. Most of that preparation is industry-agnostic, meaning that some of the information will be just as applicable in other industries as it is in consulting. First and foremost, you will want to ensure that you have done your homework. In other words, you want to prepare yourself to successfully meet the previously discussed Day 1 objectives.

To accomplish this, focus on both yourself and everything external that is of relevance. This is easier than you may think, yet some new joiners still fail at this task miserably time and time again.

Personal Aspects to Consider

First of all, you want to ensure you come across as a valuable asset to the team. Pretending won't be enough. You will have to deliver quality work, which will ultimately be the relevant measure of success. However, when you are starting out – really on your first day – this should not be your major concern. You want to focus on making a positive first impression, as it will likely be a lasting one. More specifically, you should consider your appearance, professional and personal online profiles, and your personal pitch.

Your Appearance

When it comes to your appearance, think of your first day (or week) at work as if you were going on a date. You want to look great but not overdo it.

Obviously, you don't want to go into debt just to look good on Day 1. Investing in quality items will come at a price. What follows next are the essentials, which should set you back less than a month's salary. If that still means you need to borrow money, then by all means go ahead and do so, but don't come to work looking like a car crash. You have to look smart.

The following are things you should consider.

- **Clothing:** Clothing includes suits, shirts, and ties for men, pant or skirt suits and blouses for women (shoes follow next). Nothing else is required for now, or at least it is not critical for Day 1.

  Keep things simple. Don't try to impress people just yet. Be practical. Think *House of Cards* rather than *Great Gatsby*. Fashion statements can wait. When establishing your new wardrobe, focus on items that can be easily matched with one another. You should avoid items that can only be worn in combination with one other item. Avoid limiting yourself.

  Buy at least two or three suits. This goes for both men and women. Navy blue suits work very well for most. Stay away from black suits unless you want to leave the impression that you're coming from a funeral. I personally prefer to have different colors to add some variety.

  You should also own a substantial amount of business shirts or blouses. For starters, make sure to have at least ten business shirts of good quality. The more you have, the lower the likelihood of running out of clean shirts or blouses due to a busy workweek (or weekend).

  Focus on white and light-blue shirts for now. They are the most versatile and can be combined with pretty much anything.

- **Shoes:** Just like your clothing, your shoes do not need to make any statement other than showing that you're ready to meet the client. Let me say that again: fashion statements are not required.

  It should come as no surprise that your shoes should be spotless. If necessary, give them a shine before you leave the house – especially on your first day. (*Note*: If you already own decent shoes, make sure that the heels are in good condition. If they're not, fix them.)

  Buy at least two pairs of good-quality shoes. They should match your suits. I recommend owning a pair of black and dark brown shoes. If you want to get a third pair, get another in black as you will likely use these more often. Furthermore, each pair should match with whatever belts you plan on wearing (if applicable).

- **Hair:** Get a professional haircut a week before you start. You do not want to look as if you just came from the hairdresser, nor as though you had not been to one for a while. Try to look normal. If you're completely clueless as to what this means in the consulting world, go to the career pages of your firm and check out what other junior practitioners look like.

  However, your grooming does not stop here. Given your new role in consulting, you also need to shave. To all the hipsters out there: facial hair is frowned upon. Regardless of what fashion magazines may tell you, consulting is not the right profession to sport a beard. Unless you have something very serious to hide, you have no reason not to shave. Remember, it is all about Day 1 readiness here. If you want to grow a beard, there will be opportunities to do so in the future. (You may have to wait for Movember though.)

- **Bag:** Buy a decent professional bag that you would be happy using on a daily basis. The small leather briefcase that you've seen in the movies is not the right choice. You won't even be able to use it until you become partner.

Consider anything that is durable, high quality, and can fit both a laptop (ideally, fifteen-inch screen size) and some documents. It does not hurt to go for big brands here, but don't overdo it. Bringing a brand new Hermès bag on Day 1 would be inappropriate in most firms.

In addition, think ahead and consider how you will travel with your new bag. Can you easily strap the bag on top of a carry-on trolley? If not, look elsewhere.

You will almost certainly receive a standard laptop bag, backpack, or trolley on your first day. They might be practical, but you would be an exception if you were to use those beyond your first week or two. Most people prefer using something they really like instead of what they just received for free. Furthermore, free bags have the tendency to fall apart quickly.

There are additional items you could consider giving a makeover or replacing. For now, focus on the above, noting that these constitute the bare minimum. Do not waste time and money on items (e.g., expensive pens, cuff links) that will not necessarily help you get ready for Day 1. You will have time to develop your own personal style over time, but that should not be your objective at the start.

In general, you should feel comfortable with your appearance. I understand that some people might not be used to wearing suits, but don't let this stop you. Instead, simply get used to it. If you have to, wear your outfit for weeks before your official start. Don't settle for excuses.

In case you need inspiration, go to www.mrporter.com (men) and www.net-a-porter.com (women), respectively.

Your Professional Online Profile

Before you officially start your new job, make sure you update your professional online profiles, such as those on LinkedIn or Xing. This will serve two purposes: First, your update might show up in your new colleagues' newsfeed. Nothing conveys motivation and commitment to the firm better than an updated profile stating that you are now working for that firm before Day 1.

Second, you will be adding new people to your network from the first day you start your new role. Do not put them off by stating something other than the fact that you are employed at the firm. You might think that still claiming to be a student in your profile would not matter, but you're wrong. What does that say about your diligence? What does it say about how organized you are?

Will all this matter on a large scale? No, of course not, but we are not talking about the large scale. We are talking about the building blocks for Day 1 readiness. This is one of them.

Your Personal Online Profile

In addition to your professional online profiles, you will want to carefully review your personal online profiles (e.g., Facebook, Twitter, Instagram). Spend some time and delete anything that others might deem inappropriate. This includes incriminating pictures, posts, and likes. Don't become a victim of your past.

At the very minimum, ensure that your privacy settings are such that new colleagues and future clients cannot view information that could potentially damage your reputation.

Your Personal Pitch

In the beginning, you will meet plenty of new faces on a daily basis. For the most part, you will only have brief chats. These will rarely consist of anything more than the usual welcome and perhaps a brief chat about your background, but do not come unprepared. Instead, think of an elevator pitch. Carefully read through the following questions, and think of succinct answers:

1. **Who are you?** Think: Where are you from? What is this place known for?

   These will be the most frequently encountered topics in your early days with the firm. Make them succinct and to the point, but also make sure that they are somewhat memorable. No need to be a comedian, but try to stand out with something interesting.

2. **What did you do before?** Think: Where did you study? What did you study? What type of relevant job experience have you had before, if any?

   Be clear about your educational background. If you studied something that most of your friends and relatives would not understand just by its title, think of a brief explanation to clarify your expertise.

3. **Is this your first time working in consulting?** Think: How can you prove that you have what it takes to be at the firm or that you will soon be an asset to the firm or team?

Mention any prior experience that is relevant (if any). If this is your first consulting stint, convey your willingness to learn and your commitment to roll up your sleeves and work hard.

4. **Where will you be based?** Think: Which office will you primarily be working from? If you had a choice, why did you choose that location?

Do not get too personal here. Respond by stating the place and explaining that this made the most sense in order to be close to your team or potential clients.

5. **Which team will you join?** Think: Who is your team lead? Who will you be working with? What will you likely be working on?

Do not assume that everyone is familiar with the corporate setup. Organizational charts and leadership roles change too frequently for everyone to remember or stay up to date. Therefore, provide some easy point of reference by mentioning your team lead, other key people, and key propositions.

6. **Why did you want to join the firm or the team?** Think: Why did you choose this firm, and what particularly excites you about the team you joined?

People will assume that joining their firm was the only or one of the only options you had. Given that, do not get too carried away here. There's no need to say that the firm was the best in the market . . . Be realistic. Remember, they know the company better than you.

7. **What do you hope to get out of your experience in the firm?** Think: Why did you choose consulting as a career starting point? Why didn't you start in another industry?

For now, assume you will stay around forever, even if you regard this only as an entry point into a promising career. If you cannot come up with something here – you would not have been able to pass interviews without some reason though – refer to my blog post on "10 Reasons to Start a Career in Consulting."

External Aspects to Consider

Making sure that you will be perceived in the best light possible is only the first step. Your Day 1 preparation should also include a number of background checks about your new workplace. You will have to dig deeper into who you will be working with, where this is going to take place, and what exactly you are likely to do.

Background of New Colleagues

By the time you have accepted your offer, you will have had contact with multiple practitioners. Some will have met you during job interviews, while others might have contacted you by email or phone. In short, you should have at least a handful of names of future colleagues already available.

Before your first day, make sure to have conducted some research on those people that you already know. This is not unethical but an essential ingredient to allow you to quickly click with your new coworkers. There are different ways to do this. Here is what I would recommend as the most practical:

1. Sign out from your professional network accounts (e.g., LinkedIn or Xing). You want to avoid your name popping

up in each of your new colleagues' updates about "people who have viewed your profile."

2. Do a quick Google search of each of your new contacts and see what comes up.

3. Go to the most relevant professional networks (e.g., LinkedIn or Xing) and search for your new contacts.

4. Print or save their profiles, and read them a few times prior to Day 1.

The objective of this exercise is not to stalk but to get a better understanding of those with whom you will be working. In particular, professional profiles posted online are often a good indication of how people see themselves or how they would like to be seen.

Logistics

You must not arrive late at the office on Day 1. Even if you will "only" be meeting people from HR, you can be certain that some type of feedback will be passed on to your boss (or other senior colleagues in your team). Therefore, make sure you know exactly where your new office is. Ideally, you should visit the location beforehand (use Google Street View, at least). You don't want to be late on your first day simply because you couldn't find the entrance . . .

Also, ensure that you are clear about how to get to the office building from your home and how long the trip will take.

Propositions and Expertise

Finally, you will want to check the entire service portfolio of your new team or their propositions. This is key. You will probably be slightly confused on Day 1, but prior preparation will help you settle in much more quickly.

Apart from your own team, try to get an overall understanding of how the firm is structured. What organizational units exist? What do they do? Who is in charge?

You will probably be introduced to these topics on your first day, but do not wait for others to spoon-feed you when you can get this information yourself. Just as rereading a book will often reveal new insights, this task will enable you to make better connections and, potentially, come up with better questions during the Q&A session.

All of this does not have to happen in isolation. If you can find intelligent ways to connect with your new boss or mentor, then by all means do so. Proactively reaching out before starting the job is appreciated.

For example, before joining, you could contact your boss via email asking to swing by for coffee. Chances are that you will end up being invited to some upcoming team meeting or something similar where you will be introduced even before your official starting day. This happens all the time, and you should take advantage of the opportunity.

Key Takeaways

- ♦ Make a good impression. Ensure that you appear sharp on Day 1. Don't get lazy after signing the work contract. Seek excellence in your first encounter with your new firm as an employee, too. This requires effort.

- ♦ Serve Day 1 objectives. Consider doing anything that helps other people recognize you as likeable, driven, motivated, and client-ready.

- ♦ Prepare yourself. Focus on essentials first, namely your appearance, updated professional and personal online profiles, and a succinct introduction pitch.

- Get your message across using your script. When you are introduced to your colleagues, you will be asked the same questions again and again. Make sure you nail your responses the first time around.

- Research. Conduct background checks on your new firm and colleagues. The more you learn in advance, the easier you can connect and cope with potential information overload.

Part 2

When You Start

Part 2 is all about getting things done without going mad. Chapter 3 provides specific action steps to successfully survive your first week. Chapter 4 adds to this by outlining the different stakeholders you will likely come into contact with in your first week or two, and detailing how to build fruitful relationships.

Chapters 5–10 focus on developing the specific skill set needed to actually become a resourceful practitioner. Finally, Chapters 11–13 conclude this part by illustrating how to work the system in your favor and advance your career.

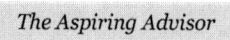

CHAPTER 3

How to Survive Your First Week

"The beginning is the most important part of the work."

Plato, *The Republic*

WHEN YOU START YOUR FIRST WEEK, you will go through a sequence of different phases. We will start by looking at what a typical kick-off session at your new firm usually looks like. Subsequently, you will have your first real encounter with members of your team. We shall review what this will be like and what can go wrong during that interaction.

Toward the end of your first week, you will have your initial practical experience on the job. Chances are your expectations will not be completely met. That's fine. We will address some of the topics that come up at this point and will specifically flesh out what you should do in your first week to establish yourself on a strong foundation in order to excel.

Induction Day(s)

Wherever you start, you will likely go through an introductory session with other new joiners. At times, these sessions may last several days or even multiple weeks. Let us briefly clarify what you are likely going to hear, who you are going to meet, and what to pay particular attention to.

The Purpose and Content of Induction Events

The purpose of induction events is to provide an overview of how the organization operates. Oftentimes, regulatory requirements will be fulfilled as well by informing new joiners about rules, professional standards, or ethical behaviors and requesting a sign-off thereof.

People You Meet During the Induction

Depending on your firm's size and hiring strategy (i.e., how often people are recruited during a year), your first day at work will likely be unique. You may be sitting in a room of ten or in a hall of three hundred. Also, do not expect to exclusively meet fellow junior consultants. Sometimes, there will be a mix of different levels (including seniors).

On the other hand, you will get to know the instructors, who are usually from the HR department, or other employees with specific expertise that will be shared during the induction session. Use these brief encounters to make a good impression. Be nice, smile, ask intelligent questions (if you have any, otherwise remain silent), and involve yourself in friendly chats during breaks.

Final Remarks on Induction Days

You will be sitting in a room full of people with a great deal of ambition. This is a fantastic situation to be in. Unfortunately, some people use induction events as self-promotion platforms. Don't be one of those people.

Do not boast about your educational merits or other details you think may impress others. You simply don't know what your relationship with those in attendance will be. Will you be working on the same project? Will one of the new joiners be your senior? Is

HR instructed to report back the new joiners' performance to each team? Don't take any risks.

So, how do you behave best? Imagine that you were invited to a friend's wedding. You are one of the guests, but you probably will not know many people besides the bride and the groom, who invited you. Using common sense, what would you naturally do in such a situation? Be open, smile, and show interest in other people.

If you do all of the above at the induction event, you will be off to a good start. The induction event is not the right platform to make lasting impressions. Settle first; excel later.

Meeting Your New Team

At some point, you will meet your new team. The team will probably be different from what you expect. Let me crush your dreams for a moment . . . By and large, every team is happy to have additional resources. As such, they will welcome you as best they can. However, "best" is usually very close to "not good."

Your team members will likely welcome you with kind words, but they are also thinking about how they can get that client deliverable out before the deadline. Here's the deal: no one says, "Hell, yeah!" when being asked to onboard new colleagues unless they have nothing else to do.

Accordingly, you will likely run through some generic checklists with a colleague on how to find your way through your new corporate world, including the intranet, knowledge exchange system (if any), time reporting, etc. For the benefit of both you and your colleague, do not waste each other's time by trying to understand all the details immediately. Be nice and cut it short. Your colleague will appreciate it.

That being said, what do you do if you really do not understand something? Quite simply, ask. However, ask other people. First, you should let your colleague off the hook and see if you can figure it out yourself (unless you are drawn onto some important work right away). If you cannot, then reach out to the people you met during the induction. They will probably have dealt with the same topics. Alternatively, you can use your gaps of understanding as a handy reason to reach out to people around you who you have not met yet. Introduce yourself, have a quick chat, and leave. After an hour or so, bring up whatever topic remains unclear and see if your newest acquaintance has the capacity to help out or knows someone who can. For more information on the people you will meet in your first few days, see Chapter 4.

Disillusionment

Chances are, there will be moments that make you doubt your decision to join the industry. I have tried to put things into perspective in Chapter 1 and argued that joining the so-called elite may not be an entirely accurate way to describe entering this industry. Now, let's look at the most common challenges that junior consultants experience in their first days and discuss what you can do to navigate your way through them.

People Are Not Available

When you first start, you might realize that you cannot meet your whole team immediately. It will probably take some time for you to meet key team members in person. Unless you are starting off on a Friday (i.e., office Fridays are common) or your start coincides with a team or firm-wide event, it will take time for you to personally meet everyone with whom you will eventually work.

As everyone should ideally be staffed on projects, only a few people will be in the office. This can be frustrating, especially if those with whom one has had contact before (e.g., during job interviews) are not available. There is very little you can do about this. Face the situation as is and make the most of it. Sooner or later, you will have to stand on your own two feet anyway. Your team is not going to hold your hand for long.

Your team will probably arrange some form of welcome for you. Even if it is just a call or an email with instructions on what to do next, you should never feel completely on your own. In the rare event that you do find yourself completely isolated, proceed as follows:

1. **Reach out to your boss and whichever team members you have met before.** Contact them by phone (or by email). Tell them that you have successfully "landed" and would be willing to offer support with whatever needs attention.

2. **Meet your staffing manager.** Introduce yourself over some coffee, tell him or her a bit about your background and your motivation, and express your willingness to offer support immediately. (For further information on how to deal with your staffing manager, please see Chapter 11.)

3. **Send a short introductory email to your entire team** unless someone else from HR or your team has introduced you within twenty-four hours of the induction session.

There is not much more for you to do at this point. Keep networking and wait for the support requests to flow into your inbox. Trust me, it will happen.

IT Equipment Does Not Work

Consider yourself lucky if you do not have any technical issues when you start your new job. Certain hiccups should be expected. There are all sorts of problems that you may encounter, including:

- Mobile phone not operable for at least twenty-four hours
- No access to the intranet for unknown reasons
- Limited access rights to the time reporting system
- Email reception only at the office, not remotely (e.g., from home)

This can be a frustrating first experience. Your team members will understand that you have technical issues that you are working to resolve, and they are exactly what you should spend your time working on.

No Project

You probably want to get on a project quickly, and that is the right mindset. In fact, you might find yourself on a client site within days of starting the job, but that is not what you should expect.

Oftentimes, junior practitioners get a little nervous in their first few weeks. They can't wait to get started with actual client work. More often than not, they raise their concerns to anyone who might listen, including their boss. That strategy, however, is not going to solve anything. In fact, this will only make you come across as bothersome.

There are many reasons why you may not be put on a project immediately. This may be due to a lack of project availability, other initiatives deemed more important that you are supposed to support, or the simple fact that you are not ready yet. Accept this reality. You cannot change it without causing trouble. Focus on what you can do right now. Everyone more experienced than you will confirm that it pays to be well connected within the firm, including the back-office support staff. Therefore, use your time at the office wisely. Stop complaining and network as if your life depended on it until you get put on a project.

"Wrong" Projects

Once you are on a project, satisfaction is not necessarily guaranteed. Oftentimes, people that get hired have clear ideas about the types of projects they would like to work on, the clients they want to support, or the industries they wish to focus on.

Enthusiasm for a project type is great to have, but the reality is sometimes different. You might end up working in industries that were never on your radar. Or, instead of supporting Fortune 500 companies, you might find yourself working with a much less prominent client. In the first two years, you should not be overly concerned about what type of work you perform. All efforts should be spent on delivering quality work and seeking as many different learning opportunities as possible.

As a rule of thumb, for development purposes, junior consultants should not be staffed for more than six months on the same project within the first two years (i.e., you should work on at least four projects in two years).

First Week Action Plan

For those who need more specific guidance on what to do when they are just starting in their consulting job, I have sketched out what potential actions could be taken throughout the first week. For the sake of this exercise, let's assume that you start on a Monday and the first day is primarily spent on the induction event. Once again, remember what you are trying to accomplish in your first days with the firm (Figure 2: First Week Objectives).

Making yourself known:
Introduce yourself using your self-introduction script/pitch.

Showing interest:
Offer your help and project a strong willingness to work.

Building your network:
Get to know people outside your team, incl. back-office staff.

Getting up and running:
Solve any remaining problems, incl. IT issues, relocation, permits, etc.

Familiarizing yourself with tools and systems:
Once you are working, there is little time to try things out. Learn about all the resources your firm offers you to get the job done now.

Figure 2: First Week Objectives

Therefore, potential actions to take in your first week include the following (Table 2: First Week Action Plan). *Note*: Any deliverables to which you are assigned take priority.

Day	Action	Comment
Monday (1)	Attend induction event Meet the team (ongoing) Meet your mentor Send introductory email to boss (if not met in person)	Limited time available on the first day. Somebody is likely going to take care of you.
Tuesday (2)	Meet staffing manager Meet secretaries Complete any follow-up tasks assigned by your staffing manager	Liaise with your staffing manager and support staff. Your staffing manager might ask you to provide some information, fill in a CV template, etc.
Wednesday (3)	Meet IT department	Meet the IT guys and make friends with them. Also try to solve any issues you have encountered already.
Thursday (4)	Meet other fellow juniors for lunch Ensure all pending issues have been resolved or escalated	Unless any other meaningful actions occur, touch base with the peers you met during the induction. Use this occasion to share first experiences.
Friday (5)	Meet team members or mentor for lunch Enter your working hours in the system (SAP or other)	Chances are some senior practitioner will schedule a lunch with you. If not, make the suggestion yourself.

Table 2: First Week Action Plan

Key Takeaways

- Settle first. Spend all your effort on quickly getting up and running in your first week. Resolve remaining issues, learn about the firm, and network as if your life depended on it.

- Don't try to impress at the induction event. Be a likeable participant and convey genuine interest. Avoid using the session as a personal platform, as this can put people off and word will get back to your team.

- Meet your colleagues but don't cling to them. Someone in your team will support your onboarding process. Remember that he or she has a day job and babysitting is not part of the plan.

- Don't give in to early frustration. The start might be different from your expectations (e.g., lack of team availability, poor IT equipment, no projects, or uninspiring projects). Trust that the situation will get better and keep learning.

- Schedule key tasks. Make a first week action plan based on your objectives (e.g., make yourself known, show interest, build your network, get up and running, and familiarize yourself with tools and systems). This will help you structure your first few days and keep you on track.

CHAPTER 4
You and the Firm

> "You can make more friends in two months by becoming interested in other people than you can in two years by trying to get other people interested in you."
>
> **Dale Carnegie,**
> ***How to Win Friends and Influence People***

A CONSULTANT'S *RAISON D'ÊTRE* stems from being able to connect with clients and being asked for help based on some type of existing relationship. For most junior consultants, this will not be relevant for quite some time. Instead, let me highlight what *is* relevant to junior practitioners.

First and foremost, you need to develop an internal network. Figure 3: Networking Landscape (essential) provides an overview of the different actors in a typical consulting organization. It is important to note that each of the different areas can potentially consist of more than one person. Given that your capacity is limited, however, you will need to focus your networking efforts on those that matter right from the start. Clearly, those with a say in your career should be your target as well as those you met during the interview phase.

After discussing your own role, we will talk through the different stakeholders in your area, which include your boss, your mentor, your immediate team, your project team, and, somewhat more broadly, the rest of the firm. For each, we will look at the person or group's role, typical challenges, perception, and expectations of you, along with ways to keep everyone happy.

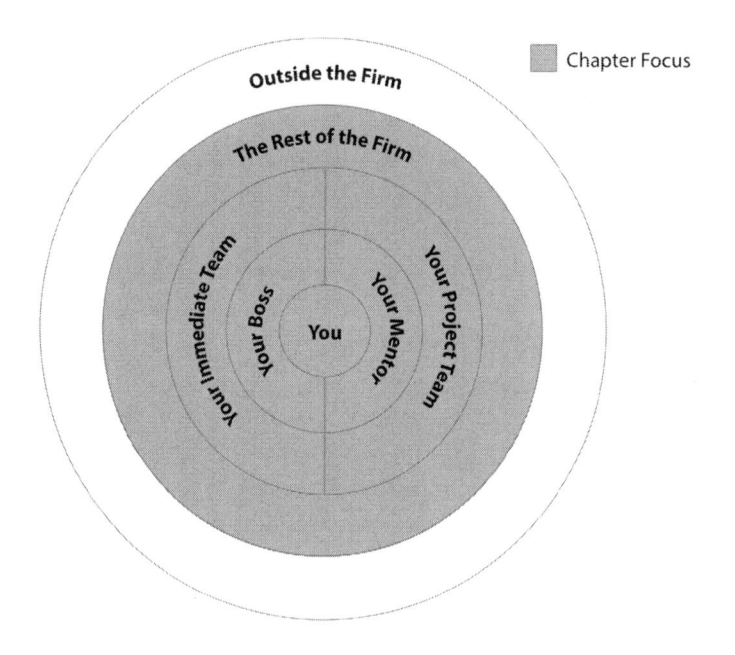

Figure 3: Networking Landscape (essential)

Starting From You

Role

Breathe and get ready for some hard truths: When you're starting out, you are essentially an unproven asset. Even if you have been hired based on a referral, you have to prove your worth to the team. It doesn't matter what you've done before. Few people care about the university from which you graduated. (Actually, no one cares, unless they graduated from the same school.) Your final dissertation will have little to no value here. Personal contacts that you may have outside the organization are also irrelevant to your professional career for the upcoming years.

You are at the bottom of the food chain. This may affect your ego. It certainly affected mine. However, on the bright side, being in a junior role puts you in the invaluable position to be allowed to make (some) mistakes and learn from them.

Don't consider any task too mundane or boring. People do recognize when junior members go the extra mile. Organize drinks? Go for it. Get the documents bound yourself? Why not? Everybody knows that it's not ideal, but someone has to do it. With the right attitude, however, it will get easier and pay off in the future.

Challenges

Your key challenges are to get up to speed and build your personal brand. However, this is easier said than done. You will need people who trust you and who will provide you with opportunities from which to learn. Over time, you will be able to develop a solid technical skill set (i.e., expertise) that can then serve as a platform to become "known" for something.

A lot of new joiners get this sequence wrong. Typically having graduated from leading schools and often having been best in their respective classes, the expectation is to excel from Day 1. The truth is, this is rarely the case, but given their ignorance, many believe that they have the right to stand for something unique and original from early on. My advice: Don't. It *will* backfire.

According to Seth Godin, "you earn the right to be heard. If there's a sick person on the plane, the doctor in 3b has the right to speak up; the hysterical person behind her does not."[4] Likewise, you will also have to pay your dues first. You have to earn your "right" to become a brand within the firm. That being said, it does not have to take long. A few stellar performances go a long way.

Key Action

In everything you do, be humble, work hard, and seek to get better every day. While doing that, keep building meaningful relationships by proactively introducing yourself and supporting those you know.

Your Boss

Role

Your boss is usually your team lead, is in charge of some distinct part of the practice, and is responsible for managing his or her own cost center. He or she is one of the most important players in your network, at least for the time being.

Your boss will be the one standing between you and good learning opportunities, either in the shape of project work or training sessions. Ultimately, you also need his or her support when it comes to promotions.

Challenges

A team lead is measured against hard, quantifiable objectives. While focus might differ depending on the situation of your firm, key criteria usually include revenue growth and profitability.

For various reasons, growing the practice is often regarded as the Holy Grail – provided that you can win project work for your team. It is a bit of a "chicken or egg" problem. In order to increase revenue, you will have to sell more. In order to sell more, you will need more people. Your boss will have to strike a fine balance, as no one benefits from a house full of idle consultants.

Perception of You

To your boss, you are both an opportunity and a burden, but you have been hired for a reason. For now, you are expected to be able to quickly add value to the team. In other words, there is hope that you will enable the team to grow and potentially help tap into opportunities that could not have been secured otherwise.

At the same time, you are a cost and a risk. On Day 1, there is only a slight chance that you will end up on a project. Why is that important? Because being on a project is equivalent to bringing in money. Occasionally, junior resources may be staffed on a project for free or for very low rates. This will allow both the junior resource and the project team to test the waters in a client environment, while clients are happy to get free resources. However, that's not the norm.

Expectations of You

You are probably not the first junior member your boss has had to integrate into the team. He or she knows the challenges and is aware that there will be a learning curve before you can become a true asset.

In order to make this happen quickly, however, you are expected to be willing to learn and go the extra mile. Finally, no one feels hurt if you also show a bit of gratitude to those people providing you with this opportunity, including your boss.

Key Action

Keep your boss happy by being willing to suck it up for a certain amount of time. Also, don't restrict yourself to those things that you think you are interested in. Early in your career, you don't fully know all of the great opportunities that exist.

One thing is certain: Things can be tough in the beginning. Whatever the challenges may be, persist. Help build the team, grow the business, and seek ways to work toward your boss' goals. Try to identify potential issues quickly and offer solutions. Nobody likes to hear a list of problems. Come up with potential remedies and offer to take care of the implementation thereof (yes, volunteer).

Your Mentor

Role

Your mentor is your guide in all career-related matters. Mind you, your mentor is not supposed to be your friend, as it is primarily a professional relationship. If the two of you can build a friendly, trusting relationship, that's even better.

Challenges

Your mentor will be a senior practitioner, and he or she will have his or her own daily business challenges, just like you. Thus, the mentor role is added to the usual workload and is not necessarily a top priority – even though that's what it should be.

Perception of You

Your mentor probably didn't pick you out of the vast pool of high-caliber junior consultants. More often than not, mentees are assigned based on a set of criteria, including:

- Which team do you belong to?
- How many levels are between you and the mentor?
- Has your mentor played this role before?
- How many mentees does your mentor already have?

As a result, your mentor will have to start from scratch in terms of getting to know you. You will likely have the benefit of the doubt, but this does not mean that you will get away with much. Your mentor will usually have a good understanding of what is required to excel in the firm. He or she will do his or her best to lead you in the right direction.

Provided that you buy in to the guidance offered, both of you will have a positive, relatively easy time. You will become like a tag team, furthering each other's careers as you go. If you do not wish to consider your mentor's advice, this relationship will not be fun for either of you, and it would be best to change your mentor quickly.

Expectations of You

You will be expected to keep your mentor aware of your development. Seek his or her counsel for everything that is work- or career-related. That being said, your actions may not necessarily need to stop there.

In order to cultivate this relationship, your mentor will reach out to you from time to time. (*Note*: Good mentors do this more often.) But don't wait for it. In fact, if you have to be asked for an update, then you have probably been a little out of touch. Don't let this happen. Instead, make it a habit to touch base with your mentor regularly, ideally in person or over the phone.

Key Action

Unlike other colleagues, your mentor will hardly ever work directly with you. Thus, he or she will likely form an opinion based on feedback from other people and yourself.

Therefore, the best way to build a trusting mentor–mentee relationship is to provide regular updates. Regard your mentor as your guardian or wingman. He or she is there to help, provided that you trust each other. That trust is built over time by sharing whatever you have on your mind and being open to feedback. For more detailed guidance on building a strong connection with your mentor, see Chapter 11.

Your Immediate Team

Role

Your immediate team is the part of your practice that will become your new home on Day 1. As such, this is your new family for the months or years to come. You will work together in multiple capacities, including on projects and business development.

Challenges

The challenge for your team is to work toward its ambitious goals (e.g., growth or strengthening of the client base). While doing that, it will be critical to keep the team happy and maintain a high utilization rate (i.e., the ratio between work on and off projects), which may require a trade-off of one over the other at times.

Some senior people may have one eye on their next promotion, potentially assuming more exposed leadership roles. Those people will have an interest in building a team. For this they need reliable people; ideally, people who get stuff done.

Perception of You

When you are new and relatively inexperienced, you will initially be a burden to some. Training any new joiner takes time, but most people understand that you will become an asset to the team if they can onboard you quickly.

By and large, new joiners are always welcome, especially by other junior-level resources, as you will help the wider team get more work done.

At the same time, there may be people who regard you as an easy target to assign tasks to. Some believe that an important part of one's development is doing "shitty" jobs; after all, they might have had to go through the same thing in the past. Others simply want an easy way out of their responsibilities and will take advantage of you.

Unfortunately, you can find people with such views at all levels, and there is very little you can do to identify them up front.

Expectations of You

Similar to your boss, your team expects you to work toward the common goals set for the group. In addition, they will want you to become a valuable member of the team and someone with whom to have fun.

Key Action

From Day 1, make an effort to get to know your team. Make yourself heard in a positive way and impress the team by delivering exceptional work and going the extra mile.

Be conscious of the fact that there will be some people who will try to take advantage of you. Do not let this stop you from giving your full effort. Instead, help these types of people once, and then stick to the "cool guys." There will almost certainly be people on the team who treat you more fairly. Stay close to them and seek ways to support them going forward. It is easier to turn down requests when you are busy with other important tasks. (For additional information on declining certain tasks, please refer to Chapter 16.)

Your Project Team

Role

It is always tricky to talk about project teams, as there is no such thing as a "typical" one. The team always depends on the project scope and client requirements. In most projects, the team is composed of a project manager and a handful of practitioners, each of whom is responsible for a certain deliverable or work stream.

Your project team is your new temporary family. Chances are, none of you have worked together before. Now is the time to come together and excel – quickly.

Some senior practitioner whom you may or may not click with will lead your team. Remember, the same thing might go the other way too. None of it should have an impact on your performance.

Challenges

The challenge of a project team is getting up and running as a group of potentially unfamiliar characters, while also managing a challenging client environment. Your project manager in particular will be under tremendous pressure. He or she needs to ensure that the team performs quickly, while also keeping the client and internal senior leaders (e.g., the partner) happy. More often than not, your project manager will privately agree with your frustrations, but don't expect this commiseration to occur at work.

Perception of You

Assuming that you have not worked with your project manager before, you will represent a risk for him or her. However, he or she will have done his or her due diligence on you (e.g., past feedback), and for the time being, your project manager will give you a chance to prove yourself. If there had been serious doubts, you would not even be on the team.

Expectations of You

No matter how challenging the project may be (e.g., a difficult client, "scope creep" [i.e., an ever-increasing project workload typically resulting from demanding clients and a poorly defined project scope], tight deadlines, poor data quality, etc.), your project manager usually has an interest in succeeding, just like you. Therefore, address potential concerns once, and then get back to work.

Your manager will then try to take care of the problem. If you really feel the need to discuss your challenges further, reach out to your trusted colleagues and your mentor.[5]

In addition, the project team will not have the capacity to hold your hand and spoon-feed you all the answers. They will be happy to assist, but they will also expect a certain level of self-motivation and initiative. Therefore, try to make life for others as easy as possible by preparing yourself in advance.

In short, your project manager only has one major expectation of you: that you do your job. Shut up and deliver . . . and don't complain until the project is complete. There will be plenty of time after it is all done to celebrate and laugh at the hardships the team endured. When the process is ongoing, however, focus on what you have been assigned to accomplish.

Key Action

Before you show up at a client site, make sure to do your homework. Make it a habit to do some research on every client beforehand. As a minimum standard, learn about:

- The client company

- The industry (characteristics, important players, trends)

- Who's who in the organization (including the C-suite and the individuals related to your project)

During the project, the first order of the day is to help your project manager by consistently producing high-quality deliverables in a timely manner. Managers do not like surprises. Make sure you agree on what needs to be done, and then meet the agreed timelines.

Furthermore, you will want to seek ways to add value to the team. For example, when spotting potential risks and issues related to the project, think of remedies first and then share your views with your manager. No one likes to hear a long list of unsolved problems. If you can provide potential solutions at the same time, what would have been a nuisance will instead be perceived as the first step toward effective risk management.

The Rest of the Firm

Role

The rest of firm represents what the term implies. It pays to have good relations with people in other parts of the firm, but, by and large, the rest of the firm's significance to you as a junior consultant is limited.

Challenges

The challenges are manifold depending on the size and structure of the firm. As such, there is nothing for you to address specifically.

Perception of You

None, unless you have already gained some modicum of reputation within the firm.

Expectations of You

None, besides not putting the firm's reputation at risk.

Key Action

Despite its relatively low level of importance to your early career, don't discard the rest of the firm altogether. Slowly establishing a network throughout the firm can help you get insights that others can't.

While easier said than done, you should focus on building relationships with people in areas that are potentially compatible with your own area of expertise (e.g., consider what may increase your likelihood of being staffed on future projects) or with whomever seems most useful for your performance review (see Chapter 13 for details about performance management).

Key Takeaways

- Build your internal network. By virtue of just having started out, there are people who will connect with you. Put significant effort into forming these relationships. They will lay the groundwork for months or years to come.

- Know yourself first. In your new job, you should fully understand your own role before anything else. Only then can you appropriately navigate the work environment and appeal to your (senior) colleagues.

- Put yourself in the shoes of your colleagues. Try to see things from their perspective. Recognize their challenges and seek ways to accommodate them accordingly.

CHAPTER 5

How to Deliver Great Work

"I do the very best I know how – the very best I can; and I mean to keep on doing so until the end."

Abraham Lincoln

A LL THE PREPARATION AND SOCIAL SKILLS in the world are irrelevant if you don't get the job done. Delivering high-quality work is essential. It is better to have a socially awkward delivery monkey on the team than someone who works the room like a politician but whose work is unreliable.

The trouble for those starting out is a lack of experience. Without guidance, it is difficult to understand what high-quality deliverables actually are. Likewise, not all people you are supposed to support should be treated equally. As a junior, however, who are you to know the difference? By the end of this chapter, you should have a clear idea of what is required and how to make it happen.

We will start by looking at the different types of clients with whom junior practitioners are going to come into contact. For each, we will highlight the key differences and levels of importance. Afterward, we will take a closer look at what quality actually means when delivering any type of job to your clients.

Finally, we will conclude the chapter with some pointers on how to produce typical examples of deliverables, including presentations,

Excel models, and minutes, in addition to making a case for learning Visual Basic for Applications (VBA).

Your Clients

Throughout this book, I refer to serving clients. For all practitioners in the industry, however, there are two distinct types of clients: internal clients and external clients. Let's look at each separately and shed some light on how to serve them best.

Internal Clients

Early in your career, your main client will most often be one of your internal senior colleagues. Some would even argue, "The most important client is the internal client." Do not let your standards slip; providing support to internal clients can make or break careers.

Internal clients can be manifold, and, depending on seniority, your priorities may have to change instantly. After all, it makes a difference (career-wise) if you provide support to the head of the firm, your respective partner, your project manager, or some other junior resource or back-office staff. Some will have a say in your future development, staffing opportunities, and promotions; others won't. Keep that in mind when being confronted with ad hoc requests, and manage them accordingly, noting that general manners and respect should guide your behavior at all times.

It is also important to recognize that changing priorities may be more common when working for internal clients. Your colleagues typically have a better understanding of what you will be able to accomplish if you are simply pushed a little more. That's just the way it is. You will end up juggling different balls in the air, and you will have to become good at it.

There are some who believe that supporting internal clients is the worst thing to do. Indeed, you will notice that not being on a project does not result in the usual downtime that one would expect. Being back at the office and fully at internal clients' disposal will likely prove to be more intense and challenging than most ordinary external client engagements (if not understaffed and poorly managed).

However, do not categorically rule out supporting internal matters, such as brand building (e.g., marketing), business development (e.g., proposals, research), or talent development (e.g., training, recruiting). Oftentimes, senior practitioners use internal work to test you in a non-project environment. As such, you should consider these pieces of work as stepping-stones to future projects by showcasing your skills and building your professional brand.

External Clients

Now, let's turn to the *real* client – the sole reason for your firm to exist. They come deliberately after internal clients, as internal clients will initially be more relevant for junior practitioners. This is not to say that junior practitioners should seek out shortcuts when on a client engagement. However, based on experience, some project managers will try to limit a junior practitioner's direct client exposure in the beginning – and quite rightfully, to protect the firm. As such, you will work for your project manager rather than the external client.

Of course, there will be colleagues who end up conducting client interviews in their first month on the job. Such situations are the exception and are likely borne out of necessity, not particular skills on the part of the junior resource.

Similar to internal clients, there is not a "typical" external client. The different types are manifold and range from the senior executive acting as a project sponsor and the finance trainee providing you the latest sales figures (which may be wrong or incomplete) to receptionists and secretaries. All client personnel have the potential to make or break a project's success. Accordingly, all of them should matter to you, irrespective of their level in the hierarchy, because what they all have in common is your professional relationship toward them. Never forget that you will always be a service provider who is paid by the client. **Be humble and seek to provide value every single day.** This is the golden rule of consulting.

A good relationship with the client is important, but ultimately, it doesn't matter how well one can connect with a client on a personal basis, because when "the shit hits the fan," you will still take the blame. Therefore, carefully consider what you say to whom, when, and how, even during more informal gatherings. You are a service provider, and, as such, you must uphold the highest standards in terms of confidentiality and professionalism at all times.

Finally, remember that not everyone on the client side will welcome you to the same degree. Some people may be more supportive of your project than others. Cooperation is key at all times, so uncooperative client personnel with some clout in an organization can represent significant hurdles to your project's success. Your project manager will (hopefully) know best how to bond with the client organization and guide you accordingly.

Having gained an understanding of the different clients and potential challenges you'll likely face, let's look at how you can actually deliver great work.

What Are High-Quality Deliverables?

As stated before, success is all about quality deliverables. Deliverables can be anything that someone will receive from you. This can range from a short email in a business context or a discussion document to financial models and final project deliverables.

I have asked both clients and practitioners what they understand quality deliverables to be. Essentially, quality boils down to three aspects: accuracy, timeliness, and design (Figure 4: Quality Components in Deliverables). Get these consistently right and you will be off to a promising career.

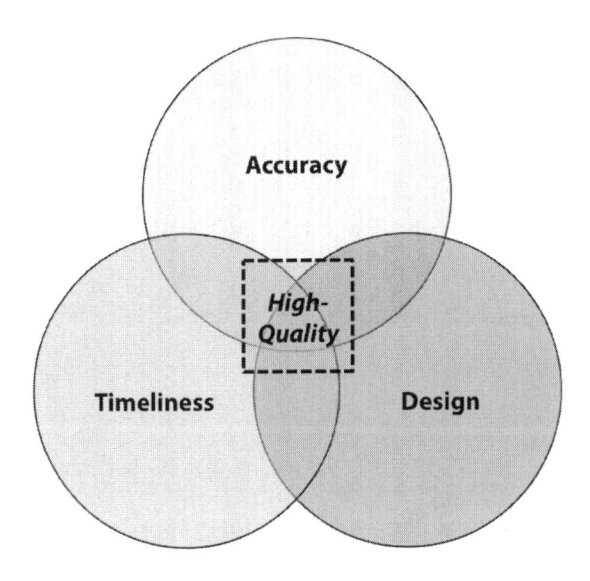

Figure 4: Quality Components in Deliverables

Let's review these quality components in order of their importance to your clients.

- **Accuracy:** Whatever you deliver, it has to be accurate. Internal and external clients alike do not have time to check your final outputs in detail. While they will do common sense checks, they also have to trust your competence.

   Before submitting anything to the client, including intermittent updates, conduct an in-depth review of your own work. For starters, you should usually focus on spelling as well as the accuracy of any calculations made. For correct spelling, make sure your language settings have been applied consistently throughout the deliverable (e.g., UK vs. US English).

When reviewing calculations, focus on totals and subtotals, if there are any. This is the quickest method to spot errors rather than calculating everything again.

Remember, paying attention to details is crucial. Imagine buying a car and finding that the rear mirror is missing one screw. How confident would you be that the rest of the car, including the brakes, was manufactured more thoroughly? The same holds true for client deliverables. Details reflect on the quality of the total work product.

- **Timeliness:** Preparation time for deliverables varies, but the vast amount of deliverables has one thing in common – you wish you had more time at your disposal.

Regardless of how much time you end up having, you will have to meet the expected deadline set by your client. If this is not feasible, you should flag that immediately, ideally up front, as managing expectations is key. No one likes surprises. Therefore, avoid agreeing on timelines that you cannot realistically work within. If you are requested to work toward such a timeline, highlight which potential changes in scope could be made.

However, once agreed, you have to meet the deadline. No exception. There is no excuse for not meeting an agreed deadline. If you need additional support, reach out to your network. Chances are, someone has the capacity to help out, or others might have done something similar before and can provide guidance that will speed up your own work.

Don't feel too proud to ask for help. Nobody can do everything all by himself or herself in consulting. Whether you need guidance from experienced business modelers (hat tip to Matt Lock), someone to challenge your thinking when you are the only resource on the project team (hat tip to Sebastian Goetz), or simply an additional hand to get stuff done (hat tip to Florian Welter), your personal network can help you. Again, if all else fails, let your manager know of your constraints promptly.

- **Design:** When speaking about getting the design right, we are usually referring to design standards and aesthetics.

First, ensure full compliance with the standard design principles set out by your client. This includes the usage of a standard template (if applicable) and consistent use of the provided color palette. You should always stick to the standards set out in the templates. Your client might still request changes that are not in line with the standards, which is okay. Just amend your file according to the updated requirements.

Second, produce only visually appealing deliverables. As with anything, "beauty" always lies in the eye of the beholder. Thus, what looks good to you might not necessarily appeal to your client. Multiple iterations will almost certainly follow. Don't get married to your deliverable or take any feedback or reiterations personally.

If your client prefers blue circles to green triangles, go ahead and change them accordingly.

After all, this is still better than what Adam in our fictive scenario, Project Bantiger, experienced with his project manager, Daniela Lopez, at one point:

DANIELA: *I don't really like this. This doesn't look nice.*

ADAM: *Sure, so what would you like me to change? What don't you like in particular?*

DANIELA: *Hmm . . . well, I don't like the color.*

ADAM: *Which color would you rather use?*

DANIELA: *(after a pause) Well, I don't know. I just don't like THIS color.*

Knowing what to generally watch out for when producing high-quality deliverables, we will now take a more in-depth look at how to actually get the job done.

Producing High-Quality Deliverables

Let's get a bit more specific about the different types of deliverables that you will encounter. To begin with, I will reiterate the importance of structuring your thinking prior to actually working on a job. We will then highlight the most common types of deliverables as well as common pitfalls.

Get Your Thinking Right

Regardless of the request at hand, before you start working, you have to step back and think through your approach to the problem. As a matter of fact, this is probably the single most important step to creating any effective work output, but unfortunately, it is often omitted.

The most common approach is based on the Minto pyramid concept. Barbara Minto, an ex-McKinsey consultant, proposes structuring thoughts as a pyramid. Thus, the main idea is on top, while supporting arguments follow underneath based on some initial hypotheses that you will test.

To avoid paraphrasing what Minto has already made available, the key advice here is for you to **get her book**. At a minimum, do some online research to thoroughly understand the concept. It might be a dry topic to deal with, but it will help you throughout your career. For further resources on structured thinking, see the Appendix.

Typical Applications and Usage

The most common tools used are Microsoft PowerPoint, Excel, and Word. Occasionally, other software will be used (e.g., when dealing with large amounts of data), but the three aforementioned programs represent what most consultants will deal with on a daily basis, regardless of their area of expertise. Table 3: Applications and Usage describes the typical use of each application and points you should consider.

Getting From Task Reception to Deliverable

It would be beyond the scope of this book to discuss in detail how all types of deliverables should best be approached. Instead, you will find a brief overview of common challenges, along with a 10-step high-level process guiding you from task reception to final delivery.

	MS PowerPoint	**MS Excel**	**MS Word**
Frequency	Very high	High/Medium	Medium/Low
Type of Use	Proposals, Project updates, Final project deliverables, Discussion documents*, Research publications	Data analyses, Databases, Project plans, Resource and financial plans*	Legal documents (e.g., statements of work, engagement letter), Final project deliverable (rare, only if requested, e.g., process handbook), Meeting minutes, White papers/reports*
Consideration		For external clients: use client template	
	Plenty of iteration, Often prepared by several people (version control essential)	Critical to think through structure from the start, Helpful if complying with design standards even if only back of the napkin exercise (may be shared with clients)	Plenty of iteration, Usually one owner, Nonacademic business writing essential

* denotes typical internal deliverables

Table 3: Applications and Usage

The Challenge

Based on my experience, a mixture of different factors represent the key challenges for junior consultants in delivering work, including:

- Unclear scope

- Last minute requests (read: limited time)

- Changing requirements of the deliverable

- Limited input from subject matter experts (SMEs)

- Additional deliverable requests

These challenges are of little concern individually. However, when taken collectively, things become tricky. You will therefore seek to cover yourself early in the process by locking in as many items as possible. The approach that works best to accomplish this is explained in the next section.

The 10-Step Process That Works

No matter how big or small the task, you should follow a standard process when you produce any type of deliverable. A structured approach can simplify the consistent development of successful deliverables. Clearly, the amount of work put into each and every step varies depending on the type of work. Follow the below sequence (see Figure 5: 10-Step Deliverable Production Process) and consider adopting it in your daily routine. Furthermore, take note of each step's peculiarities.

	Step	Comment	Involvement
1	Receive Request	Be somewhat selective. Don't jump on every opportunity. Flag any potential issues upfront.	You
2	Confirm Understanding	Avoid any uncertainties. Clarify requirements and intended timeline before starting your work.	You & Senior/Client
3	Think Through Approach	There are usually multiple approaches. Step back and think of the most practical one.	You
4	Prepare Draft	Go low tech. Step back from your machine, and prepare a rough draft using pen and paper.	You
5	Confirm Approach	Get feedback on your approach and agree on how to proceed best. Achieving agreement is critical.	You & Senior/Client
6	Execute Agreed Approach	Execute. Execute. Execute.	You
7	Provide Update	Inform client of status in person or by email, share your latest version, and request feedback.	You & Senior/Client
8	Incorporate Feedback	Visibly include the feedback points.	You
9	Finalize & Review	Dot the i's and cross the t's. Check spelling, alignment, totals and subtotals, etc.	You
10	Deliver Document	Deliver on time – not before. Ensure your work is top quality. Check wording if you deliver by email.	You

Figure 5: 10-Step Deliverable Production Process

1. **Receive request:** Be open and try to show interest when you receive a new request. Obviously, you want to avoid jumping on each and every opportunity. Be somewhat selective and don't be afraid to mention potential capacity constraints. If these are flagged up front, your client might seek out additional support or consider alternative options.

2. **Confirm understanding of request:** Once you have agreed to take on a certain task, ensure that you have a good understanding of what you are required to do. You want to be completely clear about the scope of the work and the intended timeline. If in doubt, it is always better to ask.

   You can find further guidance on how to handle client requests in Chapter 9.

3. **Think through the approach:** When you are clear about what the desired output should be, spend some time considering different approaches for how to get there. There is rarely one perfect approach. Choose the one that has the least constraints or downsides.

4. **Prepare draft structure:** Once you have decided the angle from which to tackle the problem, prepare a draft outline of your approach. Let's look at what this would mean in practice using three typical examples, namely process plans, PowerPoint presentations, and Excel analyses.
   - Process plan: You might be asked to design an execution plan for devising, aligning, and signing off the headcount enrollment plans of an organiza-

tion. Think through the different steps necessary to accomplish the task and walk your client through the process by sketching these steps out on a flipchart.

- Presentation: The request might be to prepare an update to a project steering committee. Before locking yourself up and collating all the information that you think will be required, spend some time devising a storyboard. Basically, you take a blank set of slides and assign a certain topic to each slide by using meaningful headings, also called "straplines." (See the next section on "6 Steps to Building Effective Presentations" for further details.)

- Excel analyses: You might need to analyze the pricing patterns in different geographic regions. Think through which different data inputs will be required to accomplish the job and what potential constraints may be. Finally, consider how to best design the actual data book (i.e., Excel file), also taking into account that you may have to update the file frequently in the future. Sketch this out in a short presentation, or, preferably, walk your client through using a flipchart. (See the section on "How to Develop Good Excel Models" for further details.)

It is a good idea to step back from your machine and use pen and paper for your thought process at this stage.

5. **Confirm your approach:** Align with your client in terms of the approach that is to be taken. This step is vital, and it is in your self-interest not to skip it. Present your initial thoughts and draft structure, and validate

both of them with your client. While doing so, be open to criticism. Don't get too hung up on your initial plan.

6. **Execute the agreed approach:** Once your client agrees with your approach, set out to implement it. However, don't go into execution mode before you have achieved overall alignment with your client. The only exception here may be your client telling you to get started despite some uncertainties or when you are aware of significant risks if the start is delayed.

7. **Provide updates:** While your ultimate goal is to produce the deliverable, do not become a hermit. Keep your client in the loop regarding your progress and flag potential, previously unanticipated, issues.

Note: It goes without saying that your manager should be involved throughout the process. Thus, when working with external clients, you will want to ensure that your manager has reviewed whatever will be shared with third parties.

At a minimum, provide at least one intermittent update to your client for every deliverable. This update should serve to inform about the current state of the project (roughly 60–70 percent complete) and allow for feedback from the client.

8. **Incorporate feedback:** Ideally, you will have received some constructive feedback. Amend your deliverable accordingly. Do not be selective as to what to include. Your judgment on these points is not required at this

time, as your client will look specifically for earlier feedback points upon receiving the final version.

9. **Finalize and review deliverable:** Complete any remaining parts of the deliverable, and conduct an in-depth review, including:
    - Alignment of all components (if applicable, such as boxes, headlines, and margins)
    - Consistent use of font style (type and size)
    - Spelling
    - Naming conventions
    - All abbreviations written out at least once
    - Page numbers as per standards
    - Correct subtotals and totals in calculations
    - Printability of the files (if applicable), including correct labeling of margins (date, page number of total number of pages, client logo, etc.)

10. **Deliver the final document:** When you deliver the final document, maintain the highest quality standard. Do not take shortcuts here. If you need to resort to external service providers (e.g., printing, binding), then do so. Do not ruin all of your hard work by presenting it in a less than ideal way. Content is important, but the quality of presentation also ranks very highly.

Armed with a standard process to develop most deliverables, you will be well on your way to junior consultant excellence. Before moving on to other topics, however, let me provide you with some additional guidance.

First, I will share some best practices for producing the three most common work outputs: business presentations, Excel models, and meeting minutes. In closing, you will learn about a useful, often underrated skill that junior consultants should acquire – a good command of VBA.

6 Steps to Building Effective Presentations

One of the most frequently used tools in consulting is PowerPoint. Whatever important message we need to express, we will likely put it on slides. Forget the "death by PowerPoint" notion for a moment. Presentations, if structured correctly, can actually be very effective communication vehicles.

In this section, we will take a look at how to produce presentations. There is a difference between developing a presentation for internal purposes versus one that is to be used in a client meeting. The latter is likely subject to significantly more iterations. At the end of the day, however, the fundamental production process will be very similar and consists of the following six steps (see Figure 6: 6-Step Slide Production Process).

Message	Story-board	Content	Formatting	Iteration	Stakeholder Prep
Define the purpose and single out the key message of the presentation	Develop the storyboard with the overall structure/flow of the presentation	Populate the storyboard with actual content	Rigorously abide by formatting standards	Incorporate feedback, and combine or toss slides. Sharpen the presentation by removing clutter	Liaise with stakeholders and share your work to avoid unwanted surprises later on

Figure 6: 6-Step Slide Production Process

1. **Define the purpose and single out the key message:** What is the purpose of the presentation? What is your key message? The more specific you can be here, the more concrete your first draft of the presentation will be.

2. **Develop the storyboard:** Much of what we do in consulting is about telling a story. The best message can fail to be received – or even backfire – if not properly presented in a convincing, logical fashion. To accomplish that, consultants usually work with "storyboards."

Basically, we structure our presentation like a book with multiple chapters. Each chapter is represented by at least one slide and one meaningful headline (strapline). As a complete "narrative," the storyboard should make sense. Thus, it should be clear, coherent, and ordered in a logical manner, such as chronologically (think phases or process steps), departmentally (think business units or functions), or geographically (think markets).

There are different ways of developing a storyboard in practice. The most practical approach is to use Post-it notes. Capturing each idea on a separate note makes it very easy to reshuffle the pieces until you have found an ideal structure. You can see an example of this process in Figure 7, showing my own efforts to write this book.

Figure 7: Storyboarding for *The Aspiring Advisor*

3. **Populate the storyboard with content:** With your storyboard in place, you will then have to add content on each page. The key is to be very selective in terms of what to include. Whatever text box, image, graph, etc., you use should clearly add value. There should be a reason for having everything in there.

Also, ensure that each slide really has one key message. If you can't convincingly answer your client's "So what?" question, then amend or remove that slide right away. Obviously, different clients have different styles. Some are very focused and only request the bare minimum, while others might want to be extra careful and ask you to include tons of additional material "just in case." You need to take both of these stylistic extremes into consideration.

Note: In this step, you may also want to consider what parts of previous deliverables you can leverage. You do not have to reinvent the wheel. At times, slight adjustments will do just fine.

4. **Rigorously abide by presentation standards:** At the very least, ensure that you are in line with the following:
   - Clear overall message of the presentation
   - Meaningful titles
   - Most important messages come first
   - One key message per slide, and certainly no more than two (unless your client has a liking for cluttered pages in font size eight)
   - Consistent structure of text, i.e., all bullet points to start with a verb (same tense)
   - Text and images/graphs support each other, (e.g., readers may be pointed to specific aspects of the visuals)
   - Minimal amount of text
   - Consistent structure of slides, i.e., similar layout
   - Repetitive phrases should be avoided
   - Pages that are similar in nature may be combined; repetition should be avoided

5. **Iterate. Iterate. Iterate.** Regardless of how hard you try when structuring your first draft, you will inevitably change your presentation numerous times. You will combine slides and toss out others. Feedback from

other people, as well as your own gut feeling, will help you develop a presentation that is both compelling and sharp.

You should conduct a final and very strict review of what *needs* to be included. Get rid of any clutter. Cut away until you are left with the bare essentials. This will not only reduce the size of the presentation, but will also sharpen the message. Remember, as consultants, we are meant to deconstruct complex situations and serve up our findings in manageable chunks.

6. **Prepare your stakeholders.** Once you have completed your presentation, liaise with key stakeholders and share your work. It is crucially important that you not surprise your clients. Even if you assume that they will likely agree, chances are they won't if they're caught off guard. Therefore, never publish any presentation unless you have secured a buy-in from your key stakeholder or client.

Again, don't try to reinvent the wheel when designing presentations. For starters, get a copy of a "presentation timesaver" file from your company (otherwise, use Google to find publicly available examples). More often than not, you will be able to at least draw from them for some inspiration.

When working for internal clients, you should also feel free to ask for example presentations (even on different topics). This will allow you to get a better feel for what style and structure they prefer.

For additional resources for creating effective presentations, see the Appendix.

How to Develop Good Excel Models

There are plenty of resources out there concerning how to get the most out of Excel, and most of these resources are online. The following section will not try to paraphrase all of the content that is already out there. For detailed resources, refer to the Appendix.

Instead, this section will provide some guidance on how to build good Excel models based on years of practical experience. We will cover two key questions that you should always ask yourself before building a model, a detailed review of different types of Excel models, and five modeling design principles with which you should comply.

Two Key Questions to Get You Started

Let us now look at what you should do conceptually when building Excel models. Just like any other request that you agreed to work on, don't rush ahead and start building right away. Step back for a moment and think through the following key questions.

- **What is the purpose of the model?** Oftentimes, the model will be simple and used only for some quick analysis. A core data set, simple formulae (e.g., VLOOKUP), and pivot tables might suffice.

- **Who is your client?** You will have to consider both formatting and usability depending on your client. If the model is for your own use (i.e., other people will not see it), then whatever works for you is just fine. If you are only asked to "come up with a number," then nothing fancy is required. If the output is to be formally handed over to an external client, then a top-notch model is what you will want to go for.

Based on your answers to the above questions, you will have a fairly good understanding of the scope of the model that you will have to develop. The following Excel model maturity levels will provide further guidance.

Common Excel Model Maturity Levels

Depending on both the complexity of the matter at hand, as well as the intended recipient of the model, we can distinguish between three different Excel model maturity levels (see Table 4: Excel Model Maturity Levels). Each level fulfills a slightly different objective, comes with more or less overall workbook complexity (e.g., color-coding, annotations), and requires a different degree of workbook protection (e.g., certain cells or sheets may be blocked from being modified or even viewed).

Level 1 represents the simplest model. Each higher level combines the qualities from the preceding level in addition to further elements. Thus, Level 2 is a slightly more sophisticated extension of Level 1. When you actually build the model, you will have to work your way up. You should initially focus on getting the data right before wasting time on formatting the nitty-gritty details.

	Level 1	Level 2	Level 3
User	You	Internal client	External client
Objective	Accurate data	Easy to review	Easy to use
Workbook Complexity	Low/Medium	Medium	High
Workbook Protection	Low	Low/Medium	Medium/High

Table 4: Excel Model Maturity Levels

Let's review each level in more detail.

Level 1

- Intended user: You (or peer-level colleagues)

- Objective: Accurate data

- Workbook complexity: Low/Medium

- Workbook protection: Low

- Description: Intended for your own use. Nobody else will work with the model. As such, the focus here is on getting the analysis right. It does not need to be fancy. However, remember that you might need to update the model in the future. Hence, apply modeling standards wherever possible.

- Key considerations:
  - What is the logic within the model? Does it make sense?
  - Is the data clean and relevant (e.g., fairly recent information, sufficiently large sample size)?
  - What will I have to calculate, and what will this mean for the model structure?

Level 2

- Intended user: Internal client

- Objective: Easy to review

- Workbook complexity: Medium

- Workbook protection: Low/Medium

- Description: This type of model is to be used by an internal client. The majority of people in consulting firms know how to deal with Excel. Accordingly, the focus here is not so much on ease of use, but on being able to review and validate the accuracy of the analysis.

- Key considerations:
  - Can third parties understand the mechanics of the model? Ensure the structure of the file makes sense (i.e., is ordered logically).
  - Have you documented all assumptions and data sources? The more specific and complete an overview that you provide here, the easier it is for others to reconcile your work.
  - Have you removed clutter? Anything unnecessary, including data sheets and irrelevant analyses, should be removed or sidelined temporarily. Just like in an appendix of a book, put all the nonessential information and references in the back.
  - Is your workbook easy to navigate? Can a third party immediately access the key output sheets? Just because you start working from a data input sheet does not mean that output sheets featuring the result of the analysis have to come last. Rearrange the order so it makes sense for the user.

Level 3

- Intended user: External client
- Objective: Easy to use
- Workbook complexity: High
- Workbook protection: Medium/High

- Description: This model is to be used by an external client who might not be particularly experienced using Excel. Accordingly, the model should be accurate and easy to use for clients of all experience levels. One memorable client of mine always requested that I make things "donkey-proof." Make the presentation as easy to navigate as possible by using consistent formatting, color-coding, and annotations (where necessary), and ensure that it is impossible to break the model itself.
- Key considerations:
  - Have you included a cover sheet? Just like in a presentation, add a simple yet visually pleasing cover page for your model.
  - Do you have a table of contents guiding the user? This sheet should provide a complete overview of how the workbook is structured. For ease of use, ideally, you should also add links to the different sheets here.
  - Can someone break the model single-handedly? Apply proper protection of worksheets, cells, and ranges to prevent your client from accidentally corrupting the model.
  - For larger workbooks, have you included and validated some type of dashboard incorporating information from several output sheets? Given that most clients are short on time, an overview with the key metrics can be highly valuable to them.
  - Is the file ready to be printed? You will have to change the print settings and prepare correct margins (e.g., page number, date, title).

- Does the file open on the first tab? To ensure that the recipient is not going to be lost right away by being on Tab 17, Cell W301, save the file while you are showing the first tab (ideally, cell A1). This will ensure that your file opens on the first tab in the upper left-hand corner.

Modeling Design Principles Making Your Life Easier

Regardless of the complexity of your model, there are certain modeling "dos and don'ts" by which you should abide. They will make your life easier when updating the model with fresh data and will also accommodate third-party use.

Remember the following five points, and you will be well on your way to Excel model mastery.

- **Don't hard code:** Never type numbers as part of formulas directly into cells. Not only will it be hard for you to update, but the model will also be error-prone and next to impossible for others to reconcile.

- **Always refer to one source cell:** Especially when running through different scenarios, you will want to see the effect of changing key parameters. Make sure that these parameters (e.g., sales) need to be changed manually only once. Using references to one source cell, the rest of the model should update itself automatically.

- **Apply formatting standards:** While more relevant for client-ready deliverables, make it a habit to be consistent in how you format your models. Just like any other document you create, an Excel model should be formatted consistently.

- **Separate data input and output using different sheets:** I recommend always having at least two sheets in each model, namely input and output. The first captures the data you have received or collated, while the second performs calculations and displays some results. (*Note*: It should be obvious that you can have multiple output sheets.) Make this a habit even for small analyses that only you will have to work with.

- **Do not play around with the source data:** Keep it clean. Don't change the structure by adding additional columns or subtotals. If you need to rework the data to make it useful for your analysis, arrange this conversion on a separate sheet (think of a sheet translating the original data set to something more useful). This will make your life easier when you receive an updated data set from your client.

Unfortunately, there are no resources that my colleagues and I can wholeheartedly recommend when it comes to Excel modeling. More often than not, you will have to start from a simple Google search.

A Vital Skill: Taking Minutes

One of the tasks junior consultants often perform is taking meeting minutes. While this might not sound appealing, remember that minutes are a vital tool in a business environment where different people depend on each other's decisions and the implementation thereof. Therefore, don't take this task lightly.

Minutes are a record of important discussion points, decisions, and assigned actions. As such, they serve to hold meeting participants accountable. With minutes as evidence, everyone can be on the same page.

Therefore, learning how to write minutes well is a key skill to acquire. The following twenty steps – divided into "before," "during," and "after" the meeting – will help you take useful and concise meeting minutes.

Before the Meeting

Some preparatory steps prior to the meeting can simplify the note-taking process. These include:

1. **Get the minute template.** Chances are, your firm or client has a standard template for minutes. If not, create one that fits your needs.

2. **Prepopulate the template** with all known information prior to the meeting, including:
   - Meeting purpose or name
   - Date and time
   - Meeting location
   - Meeting chair

3. **Create an outline** based on the meeting agenda. This predefined structure simplifies the process of taking notes.

4. **Understand what information will have to be captured.** This may include:
   - Complete list of attendees and those unable to attend (apologies)
   - Acceptance or amendments to previous minutes
   - For each major agenda item capture:

- » Decisions or actions taken
- » Next steps
- » Voting results
- » Parked items
- » Motions taken or rejected
- » Next meeting date and time

During the Meeting

When you are assigned to take minutes, you should ensure that you are not a major participant in the meeting. Actively participating while taking notes will be difficult.

You may want to work on the basis of your minute template or a simple outline on your notepad, which most people find easier. In so doing, keep the following points in mind:

5. **Check off attendees** as soon as people join the meeting (or telephone conference).

6. **Capture decisions** as soon as they occur to avoid losing track.

7. **Ask for clarification** if you feel that you have not fully understood a certain part of the discussion.

8. **Focus.** Don't capture meeting discussions verbatim. Instead, limit yourself to decisions, assignments, action steps, etc.

After the Meeting

Once the meeting is over, you will have to consolidate your notes and finalize them as official minutes. The following steps are essential to accomplish this:

9. **Create the draft of your minutes on the same day** the meeting was held. With the discussion still fresh in your mind, this will be infinitely easier.

10. **Review your notes** and ensure that each decision is briefly described and supported with a rationale. For lengthy deliberations, summarizing key arguments can be useful.

11. **Create an objective account** of the meeting's decisions. Don't report your personal observations.

12. **Use the same tense** consistently throughout the document.

13. **Abbreviate people's names** for larger audiences (e.g., Moritz Dressel might be "MOD" or "DRE").

14. **Limit the usage of adjectives or adverbs** as much as possible. Cut away anything unnecessary.

15. **Confirm your minutes' balance of brevity and clarity**. Edit if necessary.

16. **Attach important documents** or provide a reference to their location.

17. **Send the draft minutes to your manager** or the meeting host for approval or amendments.

18. **Incorporate feedback.** Don't expect your first draft to be perfect.

19. **Send the final version out within twenty-four hours** after the meeting to your manager (or meeting host, attendees).

20. Save your (scanned) notes for future reference.

One final point on recording meetings or telephone conferences should be considered. Sometimes, you will want to listen to parts of the conversation again. However, "taping" is very uncommon, as people tend to be more defensive and the conversation might not flow well once you have informed them that you are recording, which is what you have to do.

VBA: The Competence That Will Simplify Your Work Life

Apart from learning how to produce specific deliverables, you should do yourself a favor and learn how to use VBA. VBA, which is short for Visual Basic for Applications, is a programming language developed by Microsoft. It can be used across the Microsoft Office suite. In consulting, its usage is most common in Excel, but it has very practical use in PowerPoint and Outlook too.

You do not have to be a tech genius to figure all of this out. I'm certainly not. I wrapped my head around this topic at some point simply because I had to. Most likely, you will eventually run into issues where VBA can help you save time or help you accomplish otherwise nearly impossible tasks.

The key benefit of VBA in consulting is automation. Whatever tasks you can think of, chances are, there is a way to automate it. Quickly filtering or sorting data based on a number of criteria? Generating custom reports from large Excel models? Sending hundreds of emails to different distribution lists directly out of Excel? Automatically producing presentations from Excel models? Merging 4,000 Word documents into one? The potential benefits of VBA for consultants are endless.

VBA has a bit of a steep learning curve, but neither is it rocket science. There is plenty of material on the Internet that can help.

You definitely do not have to reinvent the wheel. Most questions have been raised before, and you are unlikely to be the first to encounter certain problems that must be solved. If your firm offers VBA training courses, make an effort to participate. You will benefit from it either directly when using VBA on the job or indirectly when trying to make sense of someone else's Excel model.

Key Takeaways

- Deliver only high-quality deliverables. Consistently produce accurate work in a timely and visually appealing fashion. Without good work, nothing else really matters.

- Think about the internal client first. Because they are key to a junior consultant's early career, you have to satisfy internal clients before external ones.

- Be swift, but don't rush. Develop your deliverables systematically. Avoid working on anything before you have agreed on the scope, timeline, and approach with your stakeholder.

CHAPTER 6

How to Master Communication by Email

"Email is familiar. It's comfortable. It's easy to use. But it might just be the biggest killer of time and productivity in the office today."

Ryan Holmes

YOU ARE GOING TO USE EMAIL A LOT, so much so that you will soon begin to hate its mere existence. Unless you have been running a one-man show in a start-up, you will likely be overwhelmed at first. The sheer amount of email messages you will receive in consulting is likely greater than what the average working professional experiences.

This chapter will show you some practical email management techniques, all of which you can implement instantly.

Explanations will be brief. This is not a detailed how-to manual. (Don't expect screenshots!) The purpose of this chapter is to emphasize the importance of the subject matter and point you in the right direction. This is meant to help you see the forest for the trees and focus on what works.

To begin with, I will establish common ground in terms of email in consulting, in general, and from a junior consultant's perspective, in particular. We will then look at adjustments you should make to your email client, including useful add-ons, to leverage its full power.

After that, we will look at handling email from two different angles. First, I will show you some techniques to manage email within your email client. Second, we will delve into how to actually write email in a business environment. We will conclude this chapter with an example email that drives home the concepts laid out previously.

Note: I assume that your company is doing all its heavy lifting by using the Microsoft Office suite. Hence, the email client would be Outlook. In the rare event that your company is not using Outlook, don't panic. You should still treat this section as critical, and do a quick search online on how to enable these settings in your particular email client.

Your Limitations

Let's get the bad news out of the way up front. Popular advice on how to manage emails is unlikely to work for junior consultants. Contrary to what you may read elsewhere, you cannot switch to checking email only two or three times a day. Likewise, switching off notifications will be impractical. As much as I would have liked to do so myself, I realized that it was simply not possible for junior practitioners.

You will be bombarded with email that is both useful and seemingly superfluous. What could be discussed and solved in a quick call is often put into an email chain. Essentially, it frees up the sender, and puts the ball into someone else's court. This is not nice, especially since junior practitioners have a hard time pushing back. Instead, you will be expected to act upon email – quickly.

With this in mind, let's look at what you can do to make your life easier with respect to email.

Essential Outlook Settings

Anything out of the box is usually not what you will want to use. This also applies to your email client, but luckily, the settings do not need to be changed greatly. A handful of adjustments go a long way.

While there are plenty of interesting solutions to get more out of Outlook, we will focus on the important stuff here. This includes folder structure, time zones, and calendar access. Set this up right now or once you realize that you should have done so earlier.

Folder Structure

The basic folder structure of Outlook is not going to be useful for your purposes. Forget about studies analyzing the effectiveness of different methods for approaching email. Given the lack of proper search functionality in Outlook and the nature of consulting work, you will want to have a minimal folder structure that reflects your current working reality.

At the very least, differentiate between internal and external email. For a time, I played around with the Archive/Follow Up/Hold folder method, but I could not make it work for me, although I would have preferred it. The approach sounds very simplistic, and simplicity is great, but I felt that this was actually bogging me down and not helping me excel at managing emails.

As always, check close to home first. Reach out to fellow colleagues to see how they structured their inboxes. By and large, the most successful individuals in your firm will use something similar to the sample below.

1. **A – Current Project:** This folder contains all incoming and important outgoing messages from your current client engagement. I deliberately added the letter *A* to ensure that this remains at the top of the folder structure while I am working on the project.

2. **Internal:** This folder includes all internal topics.

- Team updates and meetings: Regular updates from your boss and any content relating to team meetings go here.
- Events: You might be asked to provide support during the organization of some internal events. This is the place to capture all communication on that subject.
- Internal projects: Internal projects are very common. They come with different labels and can include simple research jobs, marketing activities, recruiting support, publications, etc.
- Proposals or business development: Consulting firms rely on actively working the market and responding to requests for proposals from potential clients. You will likely be asked to help out occasionally.
    » Company A – Proposal X
    » Company B – Proposal Y
    » Company C – Proposal Z
- IT: File all communications with IT here, as well as useful tools, links, and templates.
- Vacation: Critical. Have this folder capture all communication for your holiday approvals. To learn more about this topic, see Chapter 15.
- AOB (Any other business): Random corporate messages that you do not delete right away. This bucket is reserved for them.

3. **Client Projects**[6]**:** This includes all past projects, or only those considered useful, that can be kept on the side.

You add to this folder by dragging "A – Current Project" in here once the engagement has been completed, and then change the name to the client and project description (e.g., Company A – Project X). Each client folder contains the following (or something similar):

- Project setup: This includes proposals, onboarding documents, copies of the engagement contract, etc.
- Team administration: This captures all relevant information about the project team, such as CVs and hours billed, as well as – keep this low profile – team dinners.
- Deliverables: Any ongoing work for key/final deliverables as set out in the statement of work agreed with the client should be captured separately.
- Countries/business units/work streams: Depending on the nature of the project, you might want to set up additional subfolders for different work streams, countries, business units, etc.
- Other: There will be topics that you cannot anticipate, so they do not qualify for their own bucket (e.g., change of leadership announcements within the client organization).

4. **X – Archive/Sent Items:** I regularly move all sent items from the standard "Sent" folder to this specific folder for archiving purposes. This is done to free up space. Depending on your firm, you may or may not need to do this.

More Time and Different Time Zones in Calendar

This might not appear relevant at first, but anyone who has ever worked on an international engagement will appreciate the following changes to the Outlook calendar: expanding the time frames shown in the calendar and adding time zones.

In addition, you might want to consider bookmarking www.everytimezone.com to give you quick access to all time zones and corresponding times in one easy-to-find place.

Calendar Access

Assuming that this is your first job, you probably have not been provided calendar access or been granted calendar access by anyone else in the past. Going forward, however, the more widely accessible your team members' calendars are, the better it will be for everyone involved.

Some colleagues might provide access right away, but don't expect this. Therefore, be proactive and adopt the following approach. It worked for others, and it will work for you.

First, check with your colleagues. Do they usually provide access to one another? If so, ask them to provide access to you, too. If this is uncommon, check with your boss and other relevant seniors to see if they would mind providing you access to their calendars. The key here is to only do this once you are asked to schedule the first meeting involving them. However well intended, anything else comes across as creepy.

At the very least, provide access to your calendar to incoming juniors starting a month or so after you. You are basically their senior, and it is important to establish good habits when you can. This is the first time you can safely set a new standard.

The Life-Saving Outlook Add-On

If you are willing to bend the rules in your favor, read on. Apart from being quick at navigating through Outlook, you can go further and install what is probably the single most important add-on to consider: an enhanced Outlook search capability.

The best part of this approach is that there are free solutions out there, and even one-time license fees should not concern you. There are a handful of options on the market. As of this writing, I would consider one of the following three solutions:

- Live Inbox (USD 30 for a one-time license), www.live-inbox.com

- OutlookFinder (free), www.outlookfinder.com

- Lookeen (free), www.lookeen.net

If you use Gmail privately, you will quickly notice how limited the search function in Outlook is. Neither I nor any of my colleagues with whom I have discussed this are satisfied with Outlook's search functionality. It is a running joke in the industry that you are better off asking your colleagues to resend certain emails before trying to search in Outlook for them – you won't find them anyway.

How Outlook Add-Ons Actually Work

Upon starting the application for the first time, your entire email client will be indexed. Depending on the amount of email you have stored, this may take some time. I have helped senior colleagues set this up and it easily took ten minutes or more. Thus, it is highly recommended to get this up and running from the start.

The Key Features You Will Use

While these add-ons come with some social media integration, you will most likely not be using them. Additional information pulled from social media platforms is nice to have, but it's not essential. In addition, some more or less in-depth analytics about your emailing behavior are usually provided. Most of this is interesting but clearly not relevant for now.

What are the relevant features then? Why am I mentioning these add-ons here? There are at least four benefits that can have a direct impact on your day-to-day work.

> 1. **Finding email:** The add-ons help you find emails that others can't. You will get asked more often than expected to forward emails you sent in the past or to dig out an email on which you were only copied and shoot it over to your manager. Of course, all this has to happen as quickly as possible.
>
> There will be those people who cannot provide the same level of service. With any of these add-ons, you no longer have an excuse and will be able to find everything relatively easily.
>
> Search for any topic in subject lines and email bodies, or filter by sender. You can do this across the entire Outlook folder structure! Try this with basic Outlook . . . it was impossible when I last checked.
>
> 2. **Finding files:** Oftentimes, what people are really after when searching for specific emails is a certain attachment. The add-ons mentioned before also come to the rescue in this situation. You can search for file types from a specific sender or by name. Managers will love you.
>
> 3. **Retrieving contact information:** "Moritz, do you have the number from that HR lady in Italy?" Being in

the middle of something and being asked by your project manager for a number that you definitely do not have on hand is terrible, especially while he is holding the telephone receiver in one hand. Don't let that happen.

Using the Live Inbox add-on, search for any email from that respective person and see what contact details are provided. For the most part, Live Inbox will be pretty good at sifting through email signatures, but do a sense check to make sure it is not your own number.

You might think that you could find the number just as easily yourself. After all, you have to look up some emails anyway. However, most signatures are not sent internally or as part of long email chains. Searching in the traditional way just isn't reliable, so use Live Inbox or something similar instead. Remember, your manager is waiting.

4. **Analyzing your email pattern:** Both Live Inbox and Lookeen come with analytics capabilities. Most of them will be of little use for you on a daily basis, but you can still try to use them to your benefit.

   Knowing the people you exchange email with most frequently, as well as corresponding response times, can help you gauge your level of interaction with key people. Be sure to keep your boss (i.e., the person who is in charge of your promotions, unlike your project manager) in your "Top 5" of most frequent contacts, and try to maintain reasonably short response times for his or her messages.

If Your Company Prohibits Installing Software

I know that some corporate policies rule out installing unapproved software. Apart from the core applications, there is usually not much you will be relying on every day anyway. Therefore, I don't expect most corporate IT groups to even have these add-ons on their radar; hence, installation is likely not permitted. In that case, use common sense.

What are all the options you could use to get approval? Speak to other colleagues first to see if they have already installed some similar solution. Alternatively, catch up with the folks in your IT department. Approach this topic casually, and avoid written communication on the matter. They will not be very welcoming to the idea of using unapproved software – especially when questions of such generate a permanent email trail. Perhaps they are using it too, even if it is not included in the "recommended software catalogue." If you do not ask, you'll never know. For more information on how to best deal with your IT department, see Chapter 11.

If this fails, consider installing the add-on anyway. Ask for forgiveness in case someone finds fault with your approach later on.[7] Remember, at times, it is easier to beg forgiveness than ask permission.

Managing Email With Your Email Client

Even the most sophisticated Outlook settings do not guarantee that you will be able to manage the massive amount of email flooding in from Day 1. Therefore, you will want to consider improving your own email management skills.

This section covers the most important tips you should consider adopting right away. In essence, this serves as a brief introduction to daily email management techniques that can be learned and applied instantly. It is not a precise science but rather a matter of awareness, followed by the willingness to proceed accordingly.

Shortcuts

There are countless keyboard shortcuts available. Do some further research in case you feel that something is missing or just to find out what else you might adopt.

For the time being, I strongly suggest getting comfortable using the following simple shortcuts. They will help you navigate around your inbox faster and don't require an engineering degree to understand:

- Ctrl+R: Reply to email
- Alt+R: Reply to all in email
- Alt+W: Forward email
- Ctrl+M, or F9: Send/Receive all
- Alt+S: Send email

Templates

One of the easiest ways to save time managing email is to use templates. Templates can be used for all types of recurring email communication. Meeting or telephone conference invitations as well as newsletters fall into this category.

However, don't spend time searching for official Outlook templates. You need scripts tailored to your particular situation and personal style. Save some of the best content that is sent to you in your initial weeks on the job, and then try to leverage as much of it as possible while establishing your own style.

Note: Throughout this book, you will find sample scripts based on the fictive project example. You can find free, ready-to-use templates at www.AspiringAdvisor.com/bonus.

Flagging

In Outlook you can flag emails, indicating when/if you have to get back to an item or act on it. There is actually some methodology behind the flagging process, but it is not useful in practice. Thus, just mark everything with a flag and then work your way down.

What you might want to do is scan all incoming emails and immediately decide how to handle them. Delete? Archive? Immediately respond? Come back at a later point?

Deleting and archiving are self-explanatory. You simply hit the right buttons or use drag-and-drop to get the job done.

An immediate response, however, should only be considered if the task takes less than two minutes and the matter is urgent and important (for internal requests), or simply urgent (for client requests). If none of those cases apply, set a flag and get back to it later.

For all other cases (i.e., incoming email you need to follow up on), you will set a flag right next to it. Try to keep your inbox as clean as possible. Ideally, there will be flags on each line. Get back to it when you have the free time or whenever you typically clear up your inbox. *Note*: You can learn more about how to manage your to-do lists in Chapter 9.

Rules

There are many rules you can set up to handle incoming email, but none of that is truly required. There is only one rule that you immediately want to include: **the one-minute delay rule for outgoing email.** This is mission-critical and might save your career at some point.

You will run into all sorts of issues on a daily basis: missing or sending the wrong attachments, an incomplete list of recipients, incorrect text in the email body, or simply mistaking a client for an internal recipient. The potential problems are tremendous, and you will be glad that you had access to pull back an email after hitting the "send" button. One minute is usually enough for your subconscious to kick in.

Search online for "Outlook 1-minute delay" and follow the steps provided. With this in place, any outgoing email will be kept in your outbox for one minute before actually being transferred. Share this point with your colleagues. They will thank you one day.

Why shouldn't you go for an extra two or three minutes? Because of time. You don't have any to spare, especially when your boss wants some file urgently. The one-minute rule should be kept in any event. Do not play around with it. Stick to the system, even if your boss does not agree. This may be your first opportunity to push back.

Schedule Emails to Be Sent at a Future Date

At times, you have some bandwidth and you think of ways to cross off a few minor items on your to-do list. Following up on a summer event that your boss has asked you to help organize? This is the perfect time to get that task out of the way. However, you do not want to do this immediately, not only because it is not critical (as client work is), but also because you run the risk of receiving an immediate response by email or phone. This isn't necessarily a problem, but chances are that it may kill your day. Don't let that happen.

Instead, schedule your follow-up email for some later hour in the day, if not on a different day altogether (Friday afternoons come to mind). This will help you cross off items on your list while making sure that nothing of minor importance interferes with your working day.

General Thoughts on Writing Email

Now that we know how to treat email from within Outlook, let's take a look at the in-depth details of actually composing emails in a business environment. This will not be the easiest part, even if it might not appear worthy of discussion. I hope this section will make you think differently.

When to Write and When Not to Write

Email is free. Or is it? Research shows that the average business person spends anywhere between 28–35 percent of his or her workday on managing email.[8, 9] If one-third of your day is spent on email communication, we can definitely put a price tag on it. Therefore, think twice before sending email.

- Is the email necessary or could you achieve the same result over the phone, via corporate messenger (chat), or in person?

- Is the content of the email contentious, containing material that should therefore not be stored electronically?

- Is this a topic that should be informally discussed first?

What this boils down to is that you should not send email when the same objective could be accomplished by calling the recipient. You also want to limit email to those occasions where trust has been established and the topic at hand is uncontentious.

Whom to Write

Obviously, you want to limit the number of recipients of any email. Recipients should have some type of stake in the communication you send. "Stake" means that they will be affected by an outcome of your email or will have to follow up on specific tasks drawn from it.

There is one caveat to this discussion, however: When sending out emails, do not assume that your manager is too busy and should not be copied in on the email. If you have considered carefully whether your message qualifies as email, then don't second-guess whether your senior should be included in the recipient list. He or she has to be included, unless instructed otherwise.

Particularly when starting out, juniors often exclude senior people in an attempt to save them from email burden. However, you can be sure that one email will simply not cut it. In fact, this approach backfires for most juniors. You will have to establish trust first. From Day 1, despite having been hired, trust still has to be earned, which takes time. Therefore, include your boss or immediate superior at all times, unless you are asked not to.

Also, remember that some people take the sequence of recipients very seriously. Carefully consider whom to include in what order. The general rule is external clients come before internal ones, while senior recipients come before junior ones.

The Power of cc

With a minimal direct recipient list in your email, you can be more liberal in terms of whom you copy into your email (cc'ing). As a junior, you will want to get your name out there, and rather than running down the hallway naked, you want to do this with business topics. Copy everyone in cc that you can think of as somewhat relevant to the content. Err on the side of adding more and wait until you are told not to cc someone.

For email that you want to have on hand quickly, where you need to ensure everything has been delivered correctly, put yourself in the cc, too. You will hit send, and after a minute (provided you have enabled the one-minute delay), you will receive the very same email. Drag and drop this email into the folder where it belongs. This will help you keep all the important pieces together. Otherwise, you will eventually have to dig out this email from the "Sent" folder.

The Curse of "Reply All" – It Doesn't Exist

Contrary to what you may read online, the "Reply All" button is going to be your best friend. In fact, for juniors, this should be the default when responding to email. Usually, you will be at the receiving end of an email requesting some type of action. Recipients of that original email should also be kept in the loop when you are ready to respond. This includes a simple confirmation that you have understood the request made (which you will have to send) as well as any final deliverable.

If you do drop people from the list of recipients, they may start to wonder and eventually question your reliability. This might sound harsh, but the world of consulting is characterized by a culture of drive and achievement. Therefore, it does not lend itself to niceties for the pure sake of them. People treat each other respectfully but can be just as quick to find shortcomings in others.

When to Use bcc

Bcc (blind carbon copy) is rarely used, and for good reason. As a general rule, anyone you include in email communication should be visible to all other recipients, but there are exceptions.

For example, imagine that you are reprimanding a team member (unlikely in your early years). You should ensure that your team leader is in the loop, but that might not necessarily require him to be entered in the "To:" or "Cc:" fields. Such action would likely create more tension between you and the person you sought to coach or constructively critique.

Another example may be bcc'ing your mentor in an email to the project manager where you are raising important concerns about your own role on the project (e.g., when understaffed). You probably would not want to highlight to your manager that you are involving other people in the organization, especially if they are senior to him or her. However, keep in mind, should your mentor hit "Reply All," the response will go to all people on the original distribution. Therefore, refrain from using bcc unless you have a very good reason to.

Writing Effective Email

It's finally time to really delve into how to write and send emails. Before looking at a specific example, we will discuss the most important components that you should consider when sending emails, namely the subject line, the email body, and attachments.

The Subject Line

The subject line serves as the headline of your email. Make it stand out through clarity. Try to be as specific and concise as possible. An ideal subject line is characterized by the following.

- **Brevity:** Limit your subject line to between five to eight words unless it is necessary to go beyond that. This will ensure that your subject line can be read on most devices without cutting off halfway.

- **Standard convention:** People like consistency, and the more reliably you can provide that, the better it will be for you and your standing in the firm (unless you screw up in your actual work). Also, make sure to utilize commonly used abbreviations (if any).

- **Clear task:** You can add tremendous value to any recipients if you help them decide what they are supposed to do. Do not require them to actually read your email to understand that. If something is for informational purposes only, mention this in the subject line.

There are two possible objectives to achieve with your subject line in a business context. The choice between the two will depend on your situation. Common sense and some learning through experience will be your guides. These two objectives are listed below.

1. **Inform the recipient about the content of your email:** This is likely the most common mailing sent by juniors. Examples include progress updates or the submission of deliverables. Be specific and allow the recipient to understand what your email is about, such as "Project X Proposal – Storyboard DRAFT." (This email should enclose a draft storyboard, or structure, of the proposal for Project X.)

2. **Make a call to action:** This depends on the content of your email and the particular recipient. I've provided examples I have effectively used in the past.

    - **REVIEW:** Asking the recipient to review either the mailing itself or an attachment and to provide feedback (e.g., a draft presentation)
    - **REQUEST:** Indicating that a request is being made through this message (e.g., approval of vacation or training)
    - **FYI (For Your Information):** Informative content, which should be read but not (immediately) acted upon (e.g., leadership changes within the external client organization of which the team should be aware)
    - **CONFIDENTIAL:** Highlighting any piece of information that should not be shared beyond a

close group of colleagues (if any, e.g., sharing initial thoughts on organizational restructuring)

- **URGENT:** Calling for immediate attention (e.g., asking for ad hoc support or critical information)
- **LOW PRIO:** Indicating a nonurgent and only partly relevant email message (e.g., useful information for future marketing activities)

You might wonder why one could not simply use the flagging function in Outlook to indicate the level of importance before sending an email. The answer? Many people already do this. Most emails tend to be of "High Importance." This is so common that, based on my experience, most recipients have stopped using those flags as a guideline for importance. In fact, I have found that "Low Importance" emails trigger a much better response.

The Email Body

What was said about subject lines also holds true for the email body. Brevity and clarity are essential. When composing your email, always ask yourself the following questions:

1. **Is what I am writing clear?** If not, rewrite it. Minimize the amount of email ping-pong by carefully composing crystal-clear messages up front.

2. **Is something redundant?** If so, delete it. If the message could do without it, then there is no reason to include it.

3. **Am I being clear about my expectations of the reader?** Is this an informational email or am I asking

the reader to do something? Review and specify whatever could be misunderstood.

After drafting the email, you should once again confirm that brevity and courtesy are balanced. When dealing with senior colleagues or clients, seeking brevity does not mean that you can cut short on formalities, such as proper form of address and correct spelling.

In addition, you want to be very explicit about the intention of your email and **the request for the recipient**. If the recipient is to act, mention this explicitly. It is good practice to mention your expectation in the first paragraph of your mailing, as demonstrated below:

> *Hereby I am sending you the latest XYZ document for your review.*

Furthermore, **state the deadline** for when the feedback needs to be incorporated. Mention this even in the rare event that no deadline exists. This will not only allow you to schedule a follow up, but recipients will also be able to accurately register the request and get back to you in time. A commonly used phrase in closing your mailing could therefore read:

> *Your review and **feedback by Friday, October 10th**, (COB/Close of Business) will be much appreciated.*

Notice that I have highlighted some parts in bold (not underlined or italics). This is a good practice to denote key information.

One final remark: For very important email messages, ask one of your trusted colleagues to briefly review the email prior to sending. This so-called Four-Eyes Principle can help identify wrong information, missing parts, or any other aspects that could weaken your email.

Attachments

Now, let's turn our attention to email attachments. There are at least five aspects of which to be aware. Don't skip this section unless you want to be on the receiving end of angry partner calls.

- **Mind the maximum size of attachments:** Most corporate networks limit not only the size of email inboxes, but also the size of attachments.[10] If you need to exchange large files (i.e., when handing over a USB[11] key will not be an option), try to use the corporate messenger tool, the client's or your firm's shared drive, or cloud-sharing solutions. For the latter, discuss this with your manager beforehand to avoid any legal implications.

- **Consider the compatibility of file types:** Usually, you do not have to be concerned about what file types you are sending out. Microsoft Office is widely used.

    However, there is one exception – senior leadership. Leaders are increasingly using iPads to manage their day-to-day operations. "So what?" you may wonder. Try to send that "Steering Committee" PowerPoint presentation to them. Chances are that they will not be able to read it properly. Formatting might be all over the place. Don't let that happen.

    Instead, when sending files to senior leaders, think ahead and provide the file as both a PowerPoint and a PDF, and mention that you added the same file in two different formats deliberately:

    For your convenience, I have attached the presentation both as a PPT and a PDF. I hope this will be useful to you.

This will serve two purposes:

- showing you had the recipient's needs in mind, and
- avoiding someone having to ask why you attached the same file twice.

- **Limit the number of attachments:** Do not send more attachments than necessary. If there are other relevant files, mention them and offer to provide them upon request or make them available in a shared environment via a link.

- **Use standard file-naming conventions for attachments:** Never send files with cryptic file names. Recipients should not struggle to make sense of your attachments. The exact naming convention may differ for each project. Seek guidance from your project manager on this at the start of every project.

For your own purposes, ensure file names:

- Are ordered chronologically
- Are not overly extensive in length
- Do not include special characters (e.g., ~ ! @ # $ % ^ & * ( ) ` ; < > ? , [ ] { } ' ")
- Avoid spaces (hint: use underscores or dashes)
- Include version numbers (if applicable)

In Project Bantiger, a good and bad example may look as follows:

- Bantiger Project Plan for PTI-09 July 2015.ppt (bad)
- 20150709_PTI_Bantiger_Project Plan_v01.ppt (good)

- **Mention attachments in the email body:** When you attach files to your email, be explicit about them in the actual email, particularly when sending more than one file. The following two rules have worked well for others in the past:
    - Mention your files in the full text but also separate them out as lists. You should introduce your attachments starting with:

        Please find attached...

    - Mention file types in your attachment description as "PPT," "XLS," "DOC," or "PDF." The full file name is only required if you send several files of the same file type (i.e., provide file names if you sent two PowerPoint files but not if you sent one Excel and one PowerPoint file).

Good vs. Bad Email: An Example

We have discussed the pitfalls of writing business emails. Let us now compare what good and bad emails look like side by side.

In Project Bantiger, Adam has helped to develop a presentation for the project's steering committee meeting. This is an important client deliverable and the engagement partner will attend the meeting. Daniela Lopez (project manager) has instructed Adam to send the information to John Wood (partner) ahead of time. The presentation includes some recommendations based on an analysis conducted by the team.

First, we look at a poor email that Adam might write (Table 5: Poor Email Example). This showcases what some may assume to be right. Afterward, I will illustrate what Adam writes instead (Table 6: Good Email Example).

Area	Example	Comment
To:	J Wood	
Cc:	-	Where is Daniela, the project manager? You always need to ensure your project manager is in the loop.
Subject line	Fwd: Re: Draft Deck	This email can be about anything, and a partner juggling different projects will have a hard time figuring this out from the subject line.
Body	Hi,	Regardless of how much time you have, you should stick to certain formalities. Mentioning somebody's name is a must.
	In preparation of tomorrow's Steering Committee meeting, please find attached the draft presentation.	John Wood will have a hard time figuring out what client is concerned.
	More specifically, you will find: • PPT: Steering Committee presentation (DRAFT) • XLS: 2 data sets used for the presentation	Two XLS data sets have been enclosed. For clarity purposes, they should be singled out here as well.
	In case you have any questions or remarks, please do not hesitate to get back to us anytime.	Clearly, a partner can come back with change requests anytime. But it helps to indicate by what time you will need to incorporate feedback.
	Best, Adam	
Attachment	Steering Comm_08 19_v02.ppt	The PPT is missing a specific date; we could assume this has been developed on August 18. Adam is also missing a PDF version for partner use.
	20150819_Bantiger_Dataset_v05.xls 20150806_Bantiger_Other Analysis_v02.xls	The purpose of the two XLS attachments is not explained. Also, are they the right versions given that they appear to be from early August?

Table 5: Poor Email Example

Area	Example	Comment
To:	J Wood	
Cc:	D Lopez, A Mills	The project manager should be cc'd, and Adam might want to consider including himself too.
Subject line	PTI – Bantiger – STC Mtg – Deck DRAFT	This subject line is extensive, covering everything the partner needs to understand what it is about.
		John understands what client and project this email is about and that the presentation (i.e., deck) is a draft.
		Note: Steering Committee is commonly abbreviated as STC.
Body	Dear John,	Mentioned name ✓
	In preparation of tomorrow's Steering Committee meeting with PTI, please find attached the draft presentation.	This is great; we know exactly what this email is about – a steering committee at PTI taking place tomorrow.
	More specifically, you will find:	This makes it very clear: there are three files for John to consider.
	• PPT: Steering Committee presentation (DRAFT)	
	• PDF: Steering Committee presentation (DRAFT)	
	• XLS: Dataset used for the presentation	
	For your convenience, I have attached the presentation both as a PPT and a PDF.	John understands why the draft has been attached twice.
	In case you have any questions or remarks, please do not hesitate to get back to us anytime.	
	We plan on finalizing the document by tomorrow, **August 20, 2015, 10 a.m.**, to allow all participants to review up front.	Here, we make it clear when we would need feedback from John by in order to ensure that we can deliver the material to all attendees ahead of time.
	Best,	
	Adam	
Attachment	20150819_Bantiger_Steering Comm_08 21_v02.ppt	All files are easily recognizable. We know what they are about – complete with date, client, topic, and version number.
	20150819_Bantiger_Steering Comm_08 21_v02.pdf	
	20150819_Bantiger_Dataset_v05.xls	

Table 6: Good Email Example

Key Takeaways

- Reply to everything. This can be overwhelming at first, but you have to react to incoming email quickly. Whether asking for clarification or confirming your understanding, take action.

- Reply to all. When you are the recipient, make sure that everyone receives your response. Hitting "Reply All" should be your default option.

- Don't leave room for interpretation. Communicate clearly. All major email components – subject line, email body, attachments – should aid the recipients' understanding.

- Set your email client up for success. Enhance your email management capabilities by making efficiency-boosting adjustments to the settings and using third-party add-ons.

- Be efficient. Adopt email management techniques that help you get the job done faster. Shortcuts, templates, rules, etc., should become part of your standard repertoire.

CHAPTER 7
How to Master Communication by Phone

> "Not returning phone calls is the severest form of torture in the civilized world."
>
> **Marisha Pessl,**
> ***Special Topics in Calamity Physics***

ONE OF THE FIRST THINGS I LEARNED on the job was how to set up telephone conferences. In fact, this was the very first task I was given. Unfortunately, there were some minor hiccups I would have liked to avoid.

This chapter highlights the most important points regarding phone communication. First, I will give you my take on phone communication in general. This includes some best practices for making calls in a professional work environment.

We will then turn our attention to an often-used medium: telephone conferences. Here, we will look at common pitfalls and discuss how to effectively set up telephone conferences. Afterward, I will illustrate what to do, and especially what not to do, when being either host or participant to telephone conferences.

The Basics of Using a Phone

First, let us start by discussing something so obvious that it should not require any deeper explanation: calling other people. In our day and age, many people use instant messengers more often than the phone. This can become a problem, as calling someone is the best way to go in most work environments. Solving issues by phone tends to be quicker and less prone to incorrect interpretation than email, and definitely beats instant messaging for more complex topics.

However, keep in mind that personal interaction is still superior. Thus, walking down one floor and speaking in person should be considered the best option if possible, especially when on a client site.

Getting to Know Your Tools

Before you actually make the first call, you should familiarize yourself with the phone system used in your firm or on a client site. You will want to develop an understanding of its functionality.

Most likely, you will be able to retrieve the official manual from the manufacturer's website. Access it and skim through the table of contents. If you have never worked in an office environment before, you will be amazed by what you can do with modern telephones.

Given that each machine is different, no further details on navigating your phone system can be provided here. Nevertheless, try to figure out how you would accomplish the following:

- Invite a third party to an ongoing call
- Connect different parties with each other
- Forward calls
- Enter digits when prompted to do so (e.g., when you want to join telephone conferences and need to enter a

code, depending on the model, you might need to press an additional button, just like the "shift" key on your computer)

Having pointed out the basics, let's look at the actual conversational part.

Making Calls

Before you call anyone, colleagues and clients alike, write down the key points you would like to discuss. Make it a habit to prepare this not only in your head but also on paper. This will ensure that you do not lose track of your point while making the call.

Have you ever received a call from someone that included something along the lines of, "Let's see . . . there was something else . . ." What impression has that made on you? Probably not a very good one. Prepare for conversations up front and you will be seen as the professional practitioner that you would like to become.

Similarly, you want to come up with a standard opener. Never get caught searching for the right words. Come up with them once, embed them in your memory, and then focus on getting material things done. Clearly, this opener depends on your personality, but make sure it is somewhat upbeat.

Every so often, you will end up leaving a voice mail message. For some, this might be new information, but the "beep" is prompting you to leave a message. Far too often, people just end the call upon realizing that no one was going to pick up anyhow. Don't make that mistake. If you spend time calling to begin with, take the extra time to leave a message.

Leaving voice mail messages is similar to the opener discussed above. It should be a standard message that you develop once, commit to memory, and then adjust only slightly depending on the list of points that you prepared to discuss.

For example, in Project Bantiger, Adam might try to follow up with Finance Analyst Philipp Seagull regarding some sales figures he received earlier:

> Hi, this is Adam (optional: of Consulting Inc.),
>
> It's Thursday, August 6th, just after 2 p.m.
>
> I was calling to confirm my understanding of the European sales figures you sent me earlier and to clarify specifically why the figures for Eastern Europe only cover 2013.
>
> Please call me back when you are free at 0031-123-445-445. Thanks, bye.

Having set the ground rules for phone communication in a business environment, let us now turn to telephone conferences.

The Trouble With Telephone Conferences

Telephone conferences are very common in business. In fact, they have become so pervasive that some key people in organizations have entire days blocked out for telephone conferences – often back to back, and at times, simultaneously.

The purpose of telephone conferences is very similar to ordinary meetings, namely, ensuring alignment among a group of people, generating buy-in, providing updates, and deciding on potential next steps.

Unfortunately, many people do not treat meetings and telephone conferences the same way. If you are meant to be in a meeting room at 3 p.m., you will probably be there on time, just like everyone else. For telephone conferences, however, it's a whole different world. Hosts are late, attendees are late, confirmed attendees do not dial in – you name it. Let me share how you can do better and excel where many others frequently fail.

How to Set Up Telephone Conferences

It was my second day at work when my manager asked me to schedule an update call with my fellow colleagues. Maybe it was just me, but in the heat of the moment, I simply went ahead and tried to schedule the call, only to realize that I lacked any real details.

First, I was not given a list of points to include when sending out the request. Thus, I had to go back to my manager and ask for information after I had already agreed to send the invitation, which is never a good thing. From this experience, I learned that it is good practice to create a list of questions and have them answered all at once. For telephone conferences, it is important to cover the below points.

- **Discussion topics:** Clarify with your manager what the key discussion points of the call will be. If you can make suggestions, great. Otherwise, let your manager guide you.

- **Time and date:** A telephone conference should ideally be scheduled as soon as the idea is raised. With busy schedules, however, that will be a challenge. Confirm with your manager if there is a deadline for when the call needs to take place. Knowing this is crucial to lock in time slots when working with senior leaders' assistants.

- **Duration:** What is the minimum period of time required? Think in fifteen-minute increments here. Just because most email clients suggest full-hour or half-hour invitations does not mean that you should stick to them. If the objective of the telephone conference can be achieved within a few minutes, then do yourself and the attendees a favor by being brief. Clarify with your manager what to aim for.

- **Attendees:** Are there any key people that have to be on the call? Will some of them require you to check with their assistants beforehand? For example, most partners have someone taking care of their administrative tasks, and thus do not expect you to directly bother them with meeting requests.

- **Location of attendees and corresponding dial-in numbers:** Keep in mind that your local dial-in code is of little use to those calling in from other countries. Unless there is a good reason not to (and the only valid one would be that you have no international dial-in codes), carefully consider where attendees will call from and provide them with corresponding dial-in codes.

  Do not simply paste a list of numbers into the email body or, worse, attach a PDF document or insert a link to some website. Provide all codes that might be used both in the email body and in the meeting location field.

- **Clarification of which passcode and chair code to use:** Someone will be the host of the call. When you are just starting out, you probably will not have personal dial-in codes for yourself yet. Thus, the chair code for the host and dial-in codes for the attendees are likely to be provided by your manager. However, to be sure, ask up front.

In the rare event of you being asked to set up a meeting series, leverage the full power of your email client and set this up with a single invite. People like accepting invites once. You want to avoid making them accept the same invitation for different dates.

For example, at the start of the Bantiger project, Adam has been asked to schedule a weekly thirty-minute update call between the client and the project team (Table 7: Telephone Conference Invitation).

The key here is to be very specific and think from the recipient's perspective. Make it crystal clear what is expected and make joining the call as easy as possible. *Note*: You could use this example as a template for your own "telco invites." An electronic version is available for free at www.aspiringadvisor.com/bonus.

When you are setting up a telephone conference, you will inevitably run into difficulties. Some people will not be available, while others will simply not respond. Keep track of your progress and proactively provide feedback to your manager. This will allow you to cover yourself and potentially let your manager jump in if necessary.

The Aspiring Advisor

Area	Example	Comment
To:	R Brown (Project Sponsor) J Moreau (Client Project Lead) P Seagull (Finance Analyst) J Wood (Engagement Partner) D Lopez (Project Mgr.)	All those required belong to the "To:" section. Adam also needs to do this in the right order, i.e., client staff from senior to junior, internal staff from senior to junior.
Cc:	C Cho (Global CEO)	Optional attendees can be cc'd. It is not common for senior executives to dial in to every weekly update call. Sometimes, however, they wish to be kept in the loop – just like Christian Cho, who deems this project very important.
Subject line	PTI-Bantiger: Weekly Update Call: Leadership	The subject line should be short and relevant. The purpose of the call should be clear from the subject line. Here, Adam mentions the client, project, and topic.
Location	Telco – US +1 123 456 789; NL +31 123 456 789; PIN 123456#	Include all relevant information, and enable attendees to dial-in directly from the location line, as this will be right in their calendars, too. (Note: The PIN is the participant passcode.)
Body	Dear all, Hereby I am scheduling a brief 30-min. call about Project Bantiger. Please find dial-in details below. **The objective of the call is to:** • Summarize key accomplishments • Discuss next steps • AOB (any other business) **Dial-in details:** US: +1 123 456 789 NL: +31 123 456 789 Participant passcode: 123456# Chair code: Adam / 555555# In case this time does not suit you, please let me know (by providing two alternative time slots). Thanks, Adam **Contact Details** Adam Mills Mobile: +31 123 445 445 Email: a.mills@consultinginc.com	This email body assumes Adam has done his homework. Thus, the majority of people should be able to accept. You don't want to clutter up your invitation with dial-in details upfront. Save this till the end. You want to be as specific as possible. If there are certain documents to be reviewed or discussed, mention this here, too. Provide dial-in details, i.e., international dial-in numbers and the participant passcode. Include the chair code directly, or mention who will be the host. You want to require people to reach out to you in case they cannot join. Depending on your style or standing in the firm, you may request alternative time slots be provided when declining the invite. Adding your signature is key. Make it easy for people to contact you directly from the invite. This includes at a minimum your cell phone number and email address.

Table 7: Telephone Conference Invitation

Let's now take a closer look at two different telephone conference scenarios. First, I will describe what it means to be a good participant in a conference call. Afterward, I will describe what you should do when you are hosting a telephone conference.

How to Be a Good Telco Participant

For starters, you will not be expected to have much input in telephone conferences early in your career. Unless you have some expert knowledge, the sole reason for you to dial in to the call is to take notes and learn. In fact, your manager probably wants you to:

- Get an understanding of project-related topics
- Understand how different actors deal with one another
- Experience how calls can go (right and wrong)

So what do you actually do in a call when you are not expected to talk? Keep a low profile. Remain silent and do not screw up. If you wanted to, you could ask stupid questions (trust me, they exist) or be in a noisy place and fail to press your mute button. Don't! If you do, your manager will reprimand you and you may not get invited to future calls.

Instead, do what common sense suggests.

- **Dial in early:** Regardless of your schedule, as a junior resource, you will have no reason to dial in late. It is simply not acceptable. If you really cannot make it in time, let the host know in advance.

- **State your name (and potentially your office and role):** When you dial in, you are supposed to make people aware that you have joined the call. Be brief. Stating your name is usually sufficient. In case you are a complete newbie to the group of attendees, you can add which office you are from or what role you are fulfilling (e.g., in Project Bantiger).

Hi, this is Adam Mills dialing in from the London office.

or:

Hi, this is Adam Mills, currently supporting on the Pharma Technology account.

- **Be online:** As a junior resource, you will likely not be traveling, so you should have access to your computer. Therefore, by all means, fire up your corporate messaging tool (e.g., Skype for Business). Be online. Consider opening chat windows with the host (unless you are sitting next to him) and other attendees who you might want to communicate with if necessary.

- **Shut up and listen:** Yes, no questions. No remarks. Dial in, state your name, and, unless requested to speak up, say good-bye when closing the call. In case you have some crucial point to raise, check with your manager or closest colleague first, but do this on mute or by using instant messengers, text messages, or email.

- **Take notes:** You might not be asked to write anything down, but you will eventually be asked to prepare a draft write-up of the main discussion points and decisions. Even if it is an informal call, your manager might casually ask you how you understood a certain discussion point. It is better to say that you will look through your notes and realize that you have nothing important to add than not to have anything to review to begin with.

- **Be attentive – but remain quiet:** So what are those occasions where you have to reach out to contact attendees via a messaging app? Emergencies, and there are many. Someone might be having trouble getting a point across, and you might be able to come to the rescue because you have that exact project plan in front of you. Some figures might be discussed and further thought through; you can quickly fire up your spreadsheet and run through those numbers. Don't jump in and provide those preliminary results though. Forward the information to the host or your manager and let him or her decide how to proceed with the information.

  It is also worth noting that you should not attempt to multitask. Do not play with your phone or text friends while on the call. It is a bad habit, despite the fact that some managers may also do it.

In short, as a junior, you will be considered a good participant if you do not screw up and are able to support in the background, if necessary.

How to Be a Good Telco Host

As a junior practitioner, you will rarely be asked to host a call in a project-related context. In such cases, you might only be required to set up the telephone conference and open it at the appropriate time. Your manager will likely be by your side and act as the host.

Nevertheless, for some internal work, you will occasionally be required to host a call. The key here is to not take this lightly, but to instead consider this as a realistic learning opportunity. People are forgiving, especially with respect to juniors. Everyone started out at some point, so people know what it's like. Having said this, you will be remembered in a bad light if you do not meet the minimum expectations. Therefore, it is absolutely crucial to focus on a few key factors that will set you up for a solid performance. (Let's not call it success quite yet).

- **Dial in early:** Open the call at least five minutes prior to the official starting time. You do not want to realize that the line doesn't work when everyone else is already desperately trying to dial in, or worse, waiting for the host. Treat a telephone conference just like you would any other meeting and arrange yourself accordingly.

- **Start the call on time:** Once you have opened the call, people will be dialing in more or less on time (read: they rarely do). Depending on the situation, you might be required to fill some time. Use common sense here. Based on experience in past calls, there is a good chance that senior people will happily jump in and start brief conversations with each other on various (related) topics.

  In any event, never wait for more than five minutes before kicking off. Unless key people confirmed that they would be dialing in late (e.g., because they are landing at an airport) and requested that the group wait, go ahead.

- **Confirm attendance as you go:** [Beep!] "Now joining . . ." People usually do not dial in at the same time. Taking Project Bantiger as an example, Adam should jump in right away by asking:

  Hi, this is Adam. Who has just joined?

  This is a crucial aspect of hosting. Many people do not immediately state their names. (You obviously should, as stated in the section, "How to Be a Good Telco Participant.")

Write down each name or check the person off on your list of attendees. Depending on the size of the group, briefly state who else has already dialed in. This gets you talking and establishes you as the host, despite potentially being the most junior member on the call.

- **Briefly sum up attendance when officially kicking off:** Once you are ready to begin, repeat the names of the attendees once again. This allows everyone to be on the same page.

- **Repeat the objectives of the call:** Even though you will have already covered key discussion points in your invite to the call, don't expect everyone to have read it. Most people are either too busy or lazy to do it. Thus, quickly summarize what will be discussed and then get moving!

- **Let them talk:** You are the host of the call, which means that you're in charge, but just like when throwing a party at your place, you're not expected to participate in every discussion. Manage the meeting, but don't try to dominate it. Let the big guys get on with it, but be sure to keep an eye on your watch and keep the team on track.

- **End on time:** Always. Watch. The. Time. This is key! Try to finish early, if possible, and never end late. If there is a push to extend the call from some participants, make that desire public by asking the group if that is acceptable for each and every person on the call. Otherwise, you will be held accountable for making someone, for example, be late for a succeeding meeting.

- **Summarize key decision points:** Before finishing the call, thank everyone for their participation, summarize key takeaways, and highlight the next steps.

- **Send out minutes or a brief write-up:** The majority of calls will require some sort of follow up. Otherwise, what was the point of having the telephone conference to begin with? Depending on the requirements, a short write-up should be shared with the attendees within twenty-four hours of the call.

In the rare event that you have to share your screen during the call, think carefully about what other people should be able to see. Ideally, use a second screen that you use for sharing material. Alternatively (and absolutely critical if you do not have a second screen available), share only specific programs (e.g., Microsoft PowerPoint or Excel). You want to avoid other people viewing your inbox, notifications, or, worst of all, messenger windows from other people on the call. If there is one underrated career-limiting move, it is this: sharing information and content with people who were not supposed to have access to it.

In short, hosting a telephone conference is not rocket science. With some preparation (and practice), you will be able to smoothly navigate through all sorts of calls, some of which might be heated debates. As long as you are doing your homework and closely following the guidelines above, the potential pitfalls will be minimal.

Key Takeaways

♦ Learn how to use the phone. Whenever starting at a new workplace, including a client site, familiarize yourself with the functionality of the phone. At the very least, understand how to connect, merge, and forward calls.

- Prepare for every call. Always have a clear idea of what your objective and discussion points in a call will be. Use standard scripts for both the opener and voice mail messages to simplify your communication.

- Don't reinvent telephone conference invitations. Use standard templates to save time and ensure that critical information is captured.

- Don't screw up in telcos. Keep a low profile, listen attentively, and avoid hiccups (e.g., being in a noisy environment or not being on mute) when participating in conference calls.

- You have to be capable of running the show. While it is more common to be asked to take notes, junior consultants are expected to be able to host telephone conferences, if necessary. Learn from every call you attend – by taking actual notes even when not instructed to do so – and take charge when requested.

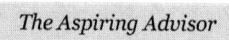

CHAPTER 8

How to Manage Meetings Effectively

> "The least productive people are usually the ones who are most in favor of holding meetings."
>
> **Thomas Sowell**

NOT UNLIKE OTHER INDUSTRIES, one thing is guaranteed: there will be plenty of meetings. While it is in our best interest to minimize the number of meetings, this is a discussion someone else besides you should have.

To help you execute properly from Day 1, we will first look at the requirements and key tasks for a junior practitioner that is helping to organize a meeting. This will be broken down into three phases: before, during, and after the meeting.

We will adopt the same approach as when you are invited to a meeting as a participant. We will conclude the chapter with an overview of meeting invitations, how to write them, and what to do when you are on the receiving end.

Helping to Organize Meetings

When you are starting out, one of the first things people will ask your support for is meeting preparation. Unless you have extensive knowledge in an area important to the meeting, your role will be to support the meeting organizer. Therefore, try to anticipate what could go wrong and take precautionary measures.

Let's look at the most important things that should be considered by junior consultants. Keep in mind, this is not just recommended by me. Senior practitioners have certain expectations of junior practitioners. If you fulfill these expectations, then you will have a successful start with your managers. Don't feel too proud to support on certain tasks. No matter how mundane the task may seem, take it, embrace it, and make the life of your manager easier. Your effort will be recognized.

Before the Meeting

Your support to the meeting host will primarily take place before the actual meeting. Your initial tasks might be of low importance to you, but they are still crucial to ensure a smooth delivery of the actual event. Make no mistake, regardless of how small, irrelevant, or below your qualifications certain requests may appear to be, consider this the price you must pay to earn your senior's trust.

Some typical tasks in this phase are finding suitable time slots with secretaries, sourcing and collating material, and booking rooms. When preparing a meeting, keep in mind the following.

- **Agree on meeting output:** You should have a clear idea of what the expected output, and corresponding requirements will be. In case of a more informal briefing, there might not be any tangible output.

  At other times, multiple topics may be discussed, decisions made, and tasks assigned. In such cases, the essence of the meeting should be documented and shared with the attendees afterward. Otherwise, it will be difficult to hold people accountable. For these cases, you will want to know before the meeting what the output is intended to be.

Also, confirm with your senior who will be in charge of writing the minutes, in what style (if unsure, ask for an example), and in what level of detail. You can safely assume that your senior is going to ask you to prepare a draft, which he or she will then review and send out to the meeting attendees. Thus, give your top effort here. (I know, these are *just* minutes, but they are critical.)

- **Confirm logistics:** Make sure you know the meeting location. Do you know how to get there? Will other people have to provide you access? Equally important, will all attendees have access or do you need to register them up front (e.g., external visitors)?

When in the room, confirm that all the equipment you will need is available and fully functioning. This includes telephones, projectors, Internet connection, felt-tip pens for the whiteboard, flipcharts with sufficient paper, etc.

Always test the material. Assume nothing! You want to avoid running from room to room to find working felt-tip pens once the meeting is underway.

- **Come prepared:** Come equipped to every meeting, however small and informal it may be. At all times, have pen and paper with you.

It is also good practice to read up on the topic of the meeting. For example, where a specific client is concerned, you will want to understand what previous work has been done with the company and who the key players are.

As a meeting organizer, you also want to have your laptop with you. You might not need it during the actual meeting if you take notes on paper, but it will come in handy when you need to project a presentation, print additional copies, or access the web or corporate address book quickly.

If there are any documents to be discussed or reviewed, take several printed copies along. You will then be able to share the material with those attendees who might not have had a chance to review the material earlier.

In case you are organizing a longer meeting (e.g., a workshop), which might involve some brainstorming or other group activity, check with your senior if a facilitator's kit will be required.

- **Have contact details for the attendees:** Whatever can go wrong will eventually go wrong. You might have key people not show up at the meeting. The group might realize that someone else should have been invited. Or perhaps some other third party should have briefly provided the latest stats or their view on an unanticipated discussion point.

  When the client executive or your partner requests you to reach out to certain people immediately, you should act quickly (and calmly). At the very least, have the contact information of all (key) attendees readily available. Access to your corporate address book and any relevant client information is vital.

- **Come early:** Be in front of or in the meeting room at least ten to fifteen minutes before the official start time. When in the room, stay close to your senior. Sit next to him or her, unless he or she tells you otherwise.

  To be on the safe side, casually tell your manager that you will go down to the meeting room fifteen minutes prior to the start, and ask if you should take something along on his or her behalf. This will demonstrate that you are thinking ahead and also offers your manager the opportunity to kindly inform you to go earlier, if need be.

- **Align with your manager:** Before you leave for the meeting, however, check with your manager on how he or she would like to run the meeting and what role you should fulfill. Don't be too proud to ask; take initiative and show that you're engaged!

During the Meeting

When the meeting starts, you will likely be relegated to a less prominent role. You may be introduced, but then again, you may not. For now, don't worry. Give your best in accomplishing the tasks assigned to you. Your time to shine will come. For now, focus on the following during the meeting.

- **Reach out to missing attendees:** You expect a certain number of people to attend. Rest assured, there will always be surprises and the group will probably be waiting for some key party. Taking care of the follow-up is the expectation for junior practitioners. Use the contact details that you have readily available.

- **Don't tighten the screws of the projector:** Most formal meetings make use of a projector. While you will likely be asked to affix the projector to your laptop, do not turn the little screws on the plug. It often happens that laptops get swapped during meetings – often unexpectedly and more than once.

- **Listen and observe:** Be conscious of what is going on in the entire meeting room. Do not get too fixated on the host and the current speaker only. As a true supporter to your senior, try to pay attention to things that he or she might miss.

If some attendees are clearly not participating and mentally checking out, find ways to include them. As this will likely be beyond your competence in the beginning (it comes with experience), a paper note to your senior will typically suffice.

Of course, this will vary depending on circumstances. Be pragmatic in your approach. As a consultant, you are meant to find solutions to problems. A meeting that is going off track is one such problem that needs be resolved. The solution does not need to be novel; whatever works is fine. The old-school paper note is a tried and tested approach that works. Be careful, however, and don't try to impress, as you can quickly be labeled as a "know-it-all."

- **Take notes:** By now, you should have an exact idea of what the required output of the meeting is. Even if you are not asked to write minutes, make it a habit to take notes.

This will not only enhance your understanding and recollection of the content of the meeting, but will also sharpen your note-taking skills for when you are actually put in charge of compiling minutes. (For specific guidance on how to take minutes, see Chapter 5.)

- **Share your printed copies:** In at least 75 percent of all meetings (approximately), some attendees will not have key documents with them. Furthermore, they have often not read critical material beforehand.

You might not officially be put in charge of doing so, but there is an unwritten rule that meeting hosts have a handful of spare copies with them. When you notice that someone lacks the required material, proactively share the copies that you brought along. Your senior and the attendee will be grateful.

After the Meeting

Organizing a meeting does not finish when the actual meeting has been concluded. For those in charge, there is more to be done once all the attendees have left.

- **Clean up the room:** Don't leave anything behind. Help clean up the room. This includes disposing of any loose papers and confidential material, clearing whiteboards (after having taken a photograph!), removing used tableware, etc.

- **Share minutes:** Depending on what you agreed on with the meeting host, you might have already been put in charge of preparing a write-up of the key discussion points and decisions made during the meeting. Otherwise, offer to prepare a write-up of the key takeaways – even if your senior might have told you differently before. Priorities may change, so your senior might appreciate this additional help now. This is also why you want to take notes at all times. You simply do not know how things will turn out.

If you are put in charge of compiling minutes, confirm with the host what the exact output format and timeline should be. You will likely be asked to turn this around within twenty-four hours.

This concludes the section on how to help organize meetings as a junior consultant. In a similar fashion, we will look at what you should do when invited to a meeting.

Participating During a Meeting

When you are invited to meetings, ensure that you understand your role as a junior practitioner. This does not mean that you come for the nibbles only. In the beginning of your career, people, particularly direct superiors, will watch you carefully. If you take the following guidance to heart without being told to "do better next time," your behavior will go down well.

Before the Meeting

Before you attend a meeting, you have some administrative homework to complete. While this will not change greatly over the course of your career, you will require less preparation time as you become more experienced. Until then, make every effort to closely adhere to the following principles.

- **Confirm logistics:** Prior to the meeting, make sure you know its exact location. Do you know how to get there?

Will other people have to provide you access? If you are unsure of these answers, reach out to the organizer or other colleagues that you trust.

- **Prepare:** Never come to a meeting unprepared. You should not only know the purpose of the meeting, but also read all documents relevant to the meeting.

- **Bring useful material:** Come equipped to every meeting, however small and informal. Always have pen and paper with you. If there are documents to be discussed, take printed copies along.

- **Come early:** Be at the meeting venue at least five minutes before the official start. As you are a junior resource, do not grab a seat right away. Remain standing until someone else has sat down. You want to avoid a) being the first one to sit and b) sitting in the wrong place.

Yes, there are wrong places. Ideally, you should ask if it is okay to sit next to someone that you know or with whom you feel comfortable. If it is a small group, sit across the table, but always consider whether very senior people are yet to arrive. You want to avoid them having to sit far away either from the group or the phone (in case other people are dialing in).

During the Meeting

During the meeting, you are probably not required to say much if anything at all. For junior practitioners, meetings are not the right platform to speak up, especially if you have nothing meaningful to contribute. However, remember that external clients are paying for you and want to get the impression that you add value, so you should do the following.

- **Listen:** Adopt an active listening style. Do not sit back and let time pass by. Instead, convey the impression that you are closely following what is being discussed. This does not require contributing more than frequent nods to the speaker and a genuine smile.

- **Take notes:** Apart from an active listening style, you want to take notes. This will not only enhance your understanding and recollection of the content of the meeting, but will also make a good impression on those keeping an eye on you.

After the Meeting

When the meeting is over, you could simply leave and get on with your own business, which is what most people do. That being said, you should try to stand out and lead by example from early on. There is no right or wrong here. The precise steps you could take depend on the context, but consider the below points and choose what makes the most sense in your specific case.

- **Leave your seat spotless:** At the very least, leave it the same way that you found it at the start of the meeting. If your schedule allows, help clean up the room. This includes disposing of loose papers and confidential material, clearing whiteboards (after having taken a photograph!), removing used tableware, etc.

- **Offer your help:** Provided that the meeting was conducted effectively, participants should have agreed on a number of follow-up actions. Seek ways to support if you can, but don't dig your own grave either. In other words, don't jump on every opportunity.

- **Connect with people:** Take time for small talk, if feasible. Again, use common sense here. Do not waste other people's time, and avoid being seen as having nothing else to do.

A Primer on Meeting Invitations

As with anything at work, you want to be efficient. Given that there are few shortcuts for juniors consultants, at least avoid trying to reinvent the wheel again and again. There is not much of a difference between sending invitations for meetings or telephone conferences, as discussed in the previous chapter.

In fact, the key differences may be whether you will have people dial in, in addition to those attending in person. If that's the case, simply add dial-in details as you would normally do in telephone conference invitations.

However, do not add dial-in details by default. You will not know who is going to attend in person and who might dial in. If people unexpectedly require dial-in details for a meeting, let them reach out to you directly.

Example Meeting Invitation

In Project Bantiger, the team has run into some initial challenges. Data quality is very poor (which is often the case) and they are struggling to find time with PTI's finance analyst, Philipp Seagull. Adam is asked to schedule a brief meeting to discuss immediate issue resolution (Table 8: Meeting Invitation).

Area	Example	Comment
To:	J Morceau (PTI Project Lead) D Lopez (Project Manager)	All those required belong to the "To:" section. Adam also needs to do this in the right order, i.e., client staff from senior to junior, internal staff from senior to junior.
Cc:	R Brown (Project Sponsor) J Wood (Engagement Partner)	Optional attendees can be cc'd. Daniela Lopez instructed Adam to cc both the project sponsor and the engagement partner. This is to keep them in the loop about potential risks. It is unlikely for them to dial in for such details, but they should be aware of them in any event.
Subject line	PTI-Bantiger: Discuss Initial Challenges & Remedies	The subject line should be short and relevant. The purpose of the meeting should be clear from the subject line. Here, Adam mentions the client, project, and topic.
Location	PTI Amsterdam, Room 251	From the location field the recipients should easily know where the meeting takes place. In the event of people dialing in. corresponding dial-in codes will have to be provided here.
Body	Dear all, Hereby I am scheduling a brief 30-min. meeting on Project Bantiger. The objective of the meeting is to: • Update on progress made and challenges encountered • Address data quality issues • Arrange additional temporary support to Philipp In case this time does not suit you, please let me know (by providing two alternative time slots). Best, Adam **Contact Details** Adam Mills Mobile: +31 123 445 445 Email: a.mills@consultinginc.com	This email body assumes Adam has done his homework and confirmed key people will be able to attend. You want to be as specific as possible. If there are certain documents to be reviewed or discussed, mention this here, too. You want to require people to reach out to you in case they cannot join. Depending on your style or standing in the organization, you may request alternative time slots be provided when declining the invite. Adding your signature is key. Make it easy for people to contact you directly from the invite. This includes at a minimum your cell phone number and email address.

Table 8: Meeting Invitation

You could use the following example as a template for your "meeting invites." I only set this up after having rewritten invites hundreds of times in my first year. I wish that someone had given me such advice earlier.

Note that as long as you have not been officially introduced, you will likely not send out the actual invitation. Meeting requests from unknown senders are usually discarded or handled with less urgency.

While setting up meetings, you will inevitably run into difficulties. Some people will not be available, others will not respond, etc. Keep track of your progress and proactively provide feedback to your manager. This will allow you to cover yourself and let your manager jump in, if need be.

When You Are the Recipient of a Meeting Invitation

If you are the recipient of a meeting request, there are a number of things you should immediately check.

1. Do you understand the purpose of the meeting request? Are the objectives and intended outcomes clear to you? If not, follow up with the organizer by replying directly and only to the sender (i.e., do not use "Reply All").

2. Will this meeting be back to back with another meeting in your agenda? If so, can you reschedule the one of lower importance?

    If both are already locked in and cannot be moved, contact the organizer of the preceding meeting (unless it is your boss, client, or other significant senior practitioner) to check whether you can step out five minutes early to allow you to attend the second meeting.

If this is not possible, because you are dealing with a significant senior practitioner, turn to the organizer of the meeting whose invitation you have just received and inform him or her that you will likely be five minutes late due to an earlier meeting.

Key Takeaways

- Don't buy into popular advice on how to avoid meetings. As a junior consultant, you are not in the position to decide whether you attend or not.

- See the bigger picture. There is more to meetings than the actual gathering of stakeholders. Junior consultants can (and are expected to) support well before, during, and after the meeting.

- Give your best in terms of meeting organization. You might not play a prominent role during the meeting, but both preparatory and post-processing work provide plenty of opportunities to shine.

- Always come prepared. Whatever the meeting is that you are attending, ensure that you have thoroughly prepared. Never take this lightly.

- Leverage what you already have. Meeting invitations lend themselves to be set up as standard templates. Only adjust dates and discussion points to save time.

CHAPTER 9
How to Manage Your Time

> "My favorite things in life don't cost any money. It's really clear that the most precious resource we all have is time."
>
> **Steve Jobs**

WHETHER YOU WORK WITH EXTERNAL OR INTERNAL CLIENTS, you will likely experience various time constraints. You will also have a hard time finding shortcuts at first. Certain processes performed at a junior level may be automated, but at the end of the day, the very reason you are supposed to perform these jobs instead of the partner is because they are time-consuming. Your partner's or project manager's time may be better spent on client management.

The question, therefore, is how to make the most of the time you have available, noting that you will have limited bargaining power and the client will (almost) always be right. In addition, you probably want to try to manage both business and private matters simultaneously. You won't be the first to do so. However, the odds are against you unless you have some simple, consistent systems in place.

This is what the following two sections will be all about: how can you navigate your work environment and deliver good quality outputs on time without losing sight of your own personal matters?

First, we will review how you can put yourself in a good position when starting a job through expectation management. We will then look more closely at how you can manage your tasks effectively in any given period of time.

The Art of Expectation Management

In order to minimize the noise directed at you, namely in the form of follow-ups and interruptions, you should establish some ground rules before working on any type of job. You will need to align with your senior colleagues on the scope of work, deadlines, and regular checkpoints. A lack thereof will backfire. So how do you go about this?

Agree on the Scope of Work

The scope of work describes what your final deliverable should include and potentially how to get there. Although it might be difficult in the beginning to estimate the actual steps necessary to accomplish a task, try to be as specific as possible with your manager. It also helps to agree with your manager about what you are not going to do in this process.

As this is so critical, project descriptions are often very detailed concerning what exactly will be done. In Project Bantiger, Adam would have two completely different starting points if asked to:

- Analyze the sales force effectiveness in Europe (poor)

- Analyze the sales force effectiveness in countries A, B, and C using sales data (including list price and discounts per item, per customer) from 2012–2015 for all sales channels (better)

Agree on Deadlines

Before starting to work on an assignment, you should also agree on a deadline. No exceptions. It does not matter if a request to you is being made by email, by phone, or in person. Always respond by asking this key question:

By when would you need this back at the latest?

The person asking for your help will often play the ball back to you. Use this to your advantage. The agreed upon deadline should be in your favor. If being asked how long it will take, do not try to impress the person by offering too short of a turnaround time. Instead, aim for a timeframe that gives you sufficient leeway in case you run into obstacles; also, be sure to challenge unrealistic expectations.

Furthermore, don't try to deliver something overnight unless it is absolutely necessary. If you receive a request by 6 p.m., you do not have to deliver the work by 8 a.m. Usually, it is sufficient to deliver by 12 p.m. the next day. This should be common sense, but I have seen many juniors and seniors forget this.

Provide Frequent Updates

You might have agreed on the scope and deadline with your project manager. Now what? Do not rush ahead and avoid updating your manager until the deadline. Your project manager will have sleepless nights unless you keep him or her in the loop. No one likes surprises (at work), especially not bad ones.

Provide informal updates either verbally (if you share a room) or by email when you have something to report. This includes both minor accomplishments (within reason) and potential challenges.

If your project manager asks you how things are going, you have failed to provide the right amount of updates. Adapt your style to your project manager. This will become easier over time. For starters, make it a habit to provide more short updates than you actually feel are necessary. Your manager can do with too many updates rather than too few. If in doubt, simply ask whether your manager felt comfortable with the amount of updates provided so as to avoid any potential criticism when performance feedback comes around.

The purpose of these updates is to inform your manager about your progress. As such, you should be completely honest about how you're doing. If you need help or more time, flag this early. Do not start on an assignment on Monday that is expected by Friday at 12 p.m. only to realize at 10 a.m. on Friday that you cannot meet the deadline.

Effective Task Management

Assuming that you have agreed on a basic understanding with your project manager regarding the scope and timeline of a certain job, you will now want to work toward accomplishing the same. By now, you also understand that priorities may shift instantly, and sticking to your personal timeline may be difficult in practice. Therefore, we shall look at some task management principles as they pertain to junior practitioners, and highlight both the pitfalls and potential remedies.

To-Do Lists and Chunking

Whatever system you use to manage your tasks, it should be simple and enable you to focus on getting things done. Your approach is not a goal in and of itself. You will want to focus on action and less on the process. Don't spend too much time thinking through your approach once you have settled on one. Otherwise, you run the risk of decision fatigue, which describes the gradual deterioration of your decision-making power.

Your mind is like a muscle. The more often you use it, the stronger it gets. However, just like any muscle, it will suffer from fatigue when used excessively. Exercising for an entire day isn't conducive to health, and it's the same with making decisions, however small. According to research from Columbia University,[12] this sort of fatigue can have a measurable impact on the quality of your decision-making skills and willpower.

So how can we accommodate this? We need a simple system to structure our day-to-day responsibilities in order to reduce the number of low-impact decisions that need to be made during the day. In other words, you want to avoid thinking, "What next?" over and over again, and save mental brainpower for decisions that matter.

In consulting, the most common method when working toward any type of goal is using to-do lists. Why? Because they are simple and they work.

Composing a to-do list requires you to come up with an action plan of how to tackle the tasks at hand. You will have to consider your approach and give structure to what might seem chaotic. Once done, however, you will rarely have to decide again what to tackle next. A list helps to minimize the number of times you have to consider any topic and thereby lowers the risk of decision fatigue.

In addition, apply rigorous chunking (or clustering) to your to-do list. Group whatever can be grouped. Similar tasks should be performed together. For example, making different calls will become a session of calls, etc.

Forget Sticky Notes...

...unless your boss is using them too. It is strongly recommended to work off paper-based to-do lists and forgo those electronic sticky notes on your computer. As mentioned before, you will have to earn trust from your colleagues. Your project team will often include someone who has not worked with you in the past. For better or worse, he or she will (subconsciously) question your reliability when getting the job done. You can mitigate this by being extremely transparent in your work. Always be willing to share your progress with your team. Paper-based to-do lists serve that purpose.

I once made the mistake of completely working off a to-do list that I was keeping on my machine. It was very convenient for me, as we were commuting between client sites frequently. However, I took a hit afterward when my performance review came around. As part of the feedback provided, I was asked to "learn how to use to-do lists." Upon questioning this remark, I learned that my project manager had not seen any to-do lists on my desk, and, putting two and two together, assumed that I had not kept any log at all.

While I did not really buy into the feedback, I immediately changed my approach and started writing down my daily to-do list on paper. Every job that required my attention and was finished got crossed off. I was very liberal in what I called a "job," because it did not really matter. The important thing was having visibly crossed off items on my list. Finished something that was not on the list before? Put it on the list and cross it off right away.

Does that sound like a lot of nonsense? Perhaps, but I have never received the same feedback since, and plenty of my colleagues have adopted a similar approach.

Schedule Recurring Events or Activities

Those people who get a lot done are usually no smarter than anyone else. They have simply structured their tasks in a way that allows them to focus. Many recurring tasks lend themselves to be scheduled on a weekly, monthly, or quarterly basis, such as:

- Entering your hours worked in a reporting system (weekly)
- Filing your expenses (weekly/monthly)

- Fulfilling compliance requirements (as required)
- Meeting with or contacting your mentor (quarterly)
- Considering professional training options (quarterly)

I recommend that you schedule these events early on. The whole process takes less than five minutes.

Split Business and Private Matters

If you have not used to-do lists for private matters until now, then by all means consider starting. If you already do this, be careful not to mix up business and private concerns. How can you effectively go about that?

Anything related to your business will take precedence unless some private matter is absolutely vital. You might disagree on that point, but that's understandable. I'm just sharing what works for me and other practitioners. Anything else is up to you.

I suggest you keep two separate to-do lists (see Table 9: Business vs. Private To-Do Lists). Ideally, you should have a different format for each. All your work tasks will be put on paper for the reasons outlined before. Your private stuff should be captured elsewhere. You will want to take the exact opposite approach with your private business and limit transparency to your colleagues as much as possible. Your project manager is not the right person to learn that you have to book flights during work hours, make an appointment with your hairdresser, or call your bank.

	Business	**Private**
Objective	Visibility Transparency	Confidentiality Privacy
Tool	Paper-based to-do list (potentially supported with task tracker in MS Excel)	Computer-based task management application (e.g., Wunderlist)

Table 9: Business vs. Private To-Do Lists

Don't get me wrong. Everyone does these kinds of things. For example, try calling a bank on the weekend . . . However, even though everyone engages in the same behavior, don't provide any potential target for cheap feedback from more experienced folks. Therefore, I recommend managing your private to-do list online. Access this list at any time from your browser. I use Wunderlist,[13] which synchronizes across multiple platforms, making it easy to manage my private to-do list on the go.

Finally, it should be clear by now that chunking is the way to go for to-do lists. What works in business matters also works well in private matters. Schedule recurring reminders to make financial transactions or take private calls.

Wherever possible, schedule those to-do items on the weekend. Keep your week free at first, unless it is an emergency (which probably would not be captured in a to-do list to begin with). You will appreciate every bit of flexibility you have maintained during a busy workday. Don't let "buying milk" get in the way of that.

A Dry Run: How to Manage To-Do Lists

Let's take a look at the concrete steps that I recommend you take when managing your different lists (see Figure 8: Weekly To-Do List

Your Weekly Routine

Every Sunday night, you will want to set yourself up for another week of success, but this requires preparation. Make it a habit (*read*: put a reminder in your calendar right now) to think ahead and consider what the key milestones of the upcoming week will be. Ideally, this will only require a short review of existing tasks that you have identified for yourself. You might need to consider certain changes in timing, but other than that, you should be ready to go. At times, however, you will derive certain tasks from new developments on a project that might not have been on your radar before. Capture those and then enjoy the last few hours of your weekend with a glass of your preferred wine.

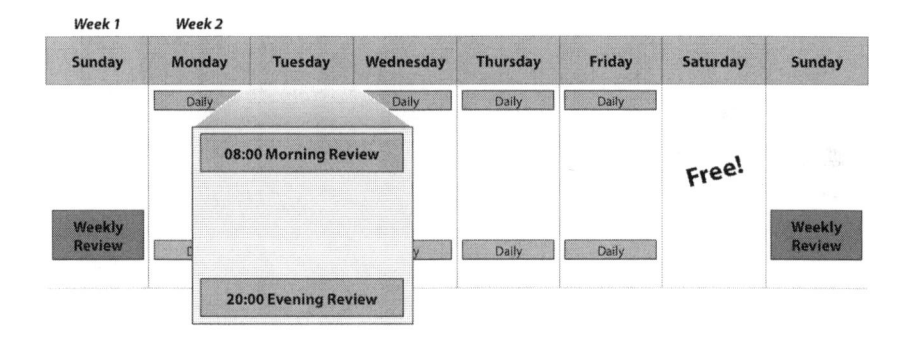

Figure 8: Weekly To-Do List Management Cycle

Your Daily Routine

Before you start your workday, you should establish a good understanding of your tasks as they currently stand and the potential challenges that might occur throughout the day. Review your daily to-do list first thing. Identify the key tasks to be accomplished and get started. Focus your efforts on the most important and urgent tasks first.

There is one caveat, however: Before thinking about work just after waking up, do something that matters to you personally. A standard morning routine, for example, consisting of exercise, reading, doing yoga, or learning a language, can lay the foundation for a happier and more productive day. Don't schedule it for "sometime later." That time will never come. It is far too easy to "call it a day" because of exhaustion at 2 a.m.

Once at work, don't sweat the small stuff immediately. These might be quick wins, but they likely don't matter in the grand scheme of things. There will be plenty of short stints of downtime during which you can take care of minor tasks. Again, this will not save you from changing course during the day, but it will help you manage the demands put on you much more easily. Before finishing the day, review your list of open items once again. Ideally, there are none, which is rare in consulting. Think ahead to the next day "at the circus" and get some rest.

Key Takeaways

- ♦ Work smarter. You have little leeway in how you structure your workday. Therefore, efficiency-enhancing time management techniques are vital to cope with typical time constraints.

- ♦ Manage your senior's expectations. Agree on the scope and deadline of a task before you get to work. Provide regular progress updates to avoid taking your manager by surprise.

- ♦ Use to-do lists. Capture all tasks assigned in groups of similar activities. This allows you to work efficiently and ensures that you do not lose track of your progress.

- Separate private matters from business tasks. Personal action items should not get in the way of accomplishing your work. Schedule them elsewhere, ideally on the weekend.

- Regularly review your to-do lists. Conduct weekly reviews on Sunday to plan the upcoming week. Every day, review the tasks for that day in the morning and when closing the day so that you remain on top of things.

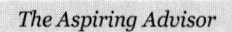

CHAPTER 10
How to Stay Ahead

"The biggest room in the world is the room for improvement."

Anonymous

WHEN YOU START IN CONSULTING, you might have just graduated from one of the major business schools. Chances are, you were also at the top of your class. If you think that after years of learning, you can now focus on practically applying your knowledge, I've got bad news for you: the real learning starts now.

In this chapter, I will highlight why continuous learning is not just a fancy concept in textbooks and why it matters in consulting more than one might think. I will describe the different roads you can take to enhance your skill set and will provide you with what I regard as the two most important daily habits to succeed.

The Case for Continuous Learning

Why do clients hire consulting firms? Because they have a need they want to address. Put a different way, consultants fill a gap that clients could not fill themselves. Conceptually, all of these needs fall into one of three categories: resources, mandate, and expertise (see Figure 9: Client Needs and Knowledge Required).

Let's discuss those categories in ascending order of their relevance to continuous learning. By the third category, you should understand that there is no way around continuing to develop your knowledge and expand your skills.

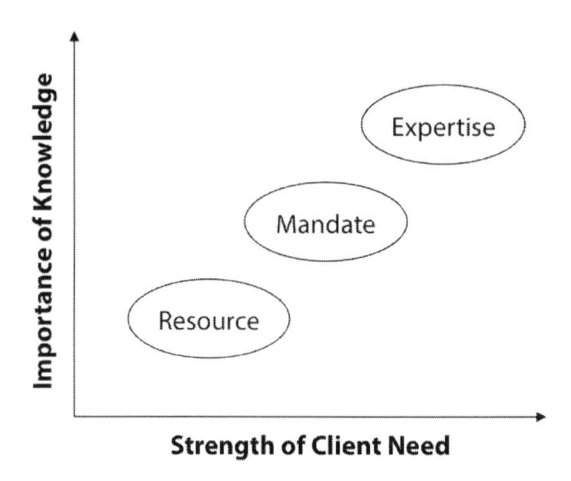

Figure 9: Client Needs and Knowledge Required

1. **Resource:** Clients might have the right competencies and know what to do but simultaneously lack the resources to execute certain initiatives. Employees usually fulfill clearly defined roles. Therefore, shifting resources without risking the structure and functionality of the entire company is a challenge. You can assign people to some new internal project, but what about the existing tasks? Eventually, one or the other has to give. Thus, clients are often faced with a simple resource issue.

They could hire staff members to fill the gap, but will they find the right candidate quickly? How long will the onboarding process take? What do you do with the resource once the task has been accomplished?

2. **Mandate:** Clients may also hire consultants to execute initiatives. They might know what should happen, but they either lack the experience and knowledge to get it done or feel that third parties, when properly mandated,[14] are in a better position to break through internal resistance.

   An employee might be able to accomplish the same task, but this person might be "burned" in the process, at which point his or her future in the company is limited. What is required is not just the ability to get the job done, but also the political savvy and ability to garner organizational support. All of this comes with experience and, above all, independence.

3. **Expertise:** At times, however, clients simply do not know what to do. This is the third classic example where consulting can come to the rescue. What external service providers can contribute in contrast to most internal client resources is much broader industry experience, significantly greater exposure to different corporate challenges, and experience in finding solutions thereof as well as deep expertise in best practices (including technology, processes, or others).

In short, clients engage consulting firms to help them by providing temporary highly skilled labor, innovative solutions, and deep industry expertise. Thus, gaining experience and developing expertise are essential in order for you to be valuable to any client.

Experience can only be gained over time and depends on being exposed to different projects. What you can directly influence, however, is the knowledge that you acquire on your own. Continuous learning is not just a fancy term; it is the very foundation of your job's future. Today's learning is tomorrow's reward. Or, closer to home, what you learn today will get you on a new project tomorrow.

Resources Available to You

Given the importance of a skilled workforce, consulting firms provide all sorts of learning opportunities. Granted, few things are more useful than practical learning on the job, but even when you are not on a project (or in your free time), you have plenty of learning resources, both internal and external, to select from.

Internal Resources

Internal resources are all those knowledge resources you can access via your corporate network. At times, there are restrictions (e.g., eligibility for certain levels only), but for the most part, they are all there and ready for you to grasp when you choose to spend time on them.

- **Internal course catalogue:** Almost all firms offer regular courses for their staff. These are often grade-specific and are either run by senior practitioners or external facilitators. The courses offered can be anywhere between two hours and multiple days, and will likely focus on one of the following.
    - Skill acquisition: Anything from structured thinking, presentation design, business writing, and financial modeling to client interviewing and programming. This is particularly valuable for those starting out (you!), as they lay the professional foundation that practitioners will be working from going forward.
    - Industry-specific training: Often targeted at more senior practitioners or those who will likely work in

a specific industry by way of prior experience, team focus, or interest.

- **Online courses:** Almost all major players in the industry provide their employees with a vast amount of online trainings via the company's intranet. Again, content ranges from professional skill development to enhancing industry-specific knowledge.

  As some of the material may be a bit dated at times, it is probably best to ask more experienced colleagues or people from the learning team (if available) for their recommendations.

  However, don't expect too much feedback. Instead, collate your own findings and share them with others later on. Also, be sure to let your mentor know. Trust me, it will pay off in the long run.

- **Knowledge-sharing platform:** The reason why consulting firms are hired is because they have an extensive arsenal of project experience and research that can be tapped into. Practitioners typically have access to some shared knowledge repository containing information about past projects (e.g., sample deliverables). Most of this will be cleansed, meaning that anything that can be traced back to the client (name, logo, color schemes, etc.) has been removed.

  Not all the information will be relevant, but you can often learn a thing or two about how others have solved a certain problem that you are facing. In case your company does not share knowledge systematically, try to initiate and implement some type of knowledge-sharing system for your own team.

External Resources

External resources are all those knowledge resources that are outside your corporate network. As such, you will have to do initial research yourself and, most likely, invest some of your personal time.

However, this does not mean that you will not get reimbursed or receive some support from your employer. There is always a chance to negotiate something, provided that 1) you ask (most people fail here) and 2) you can clearly articulate the benefit for the firm.

- **Newspapers and magazines:** Scan the news every day. You do not need to study everything in depth, but make sure that you have a solid understanding of what is happening in the "real" world, especially with the latest market developments, your current client, and their corresponding industry. (*Note:* You can subscribe to professional feeds covering clients and industries via most corporate networks.)

- **Books:** Books are the most accessible knowledge resource you can utilize. Standing on the shoulders of giants has never been easier since books are now available in formats for all tastes (print, e-book, audiobook).

Make it a habit to keep a reading list at all times. If you do not know where to start, order the five most relevant books in the professional field you are starting in right now and work your way through them over the next few weeks. Do not let a month pass without having read a new book (no matter how busy and intense your schedule may be).

If that is too difficult, sign up with www.getabstract.com. For less than the cost of a nice dinner for two, you will get a year's worth of access to thousands of concise summaries of both classic and recent publications. You might also want to check whether your employer has a corporate account with this sort of platform that is available for employees.

- **Online resources:** These days, there is next to nothing that you can't learn via the Internet. Whatever obscure interest you may have, there is bound to be a community of enthusiasts online.

The easiest starting point remains YouTube.com, especially when it comes to how-to pieces related to technical skills. YouTube almost always has some useful information to get you started.

TED Talks are another useful source of information. While they may not help you solve immediate technical problems, they can still broaden your horizons and sharpen your thinking. Make it a habit to regularly watch TED Talks at www.ted.com when you have downtime (e.g., during breakfast or dinner).

If you are looking for more in-depth courses online, check out Udemy.com. There, you can find information on anything from office productivity (Office, SAP, SalesForce, etc.), project management, and data analytics to

IT certifications and more. Selecting from the 20,000+ courses is the hardest part.

- **Other external professional courses:** Every once in a while you might realize that your corporate network does not provide training on a certain topic. If you consider this critical to your own development, conduct some research on who delivers this type of training and at what price point you could join. With thorough information and a clear case for why a training is business-critical, you can discuss and agree on the next steps with your mentor.

Do not simply rush ahead and put this on your boss's agenda. Your mentor can guide you in terms of the best approach and might show you funding options of which you had been unaware.

In case you can't secure funding from your firm, consider whether it makes sense to go ahead and personally pay for the training anyway. In the rush of daily project life, training often gets forgotten or deprioritized. Don't let this happen to you. Remember, today's learning will lead to tomorrow's reward.

How to Truly Stay Ahead

By now, you can probably appreciate why continuous learning is the name of game when working in consulting. It is the very foundation of your work. You will also have gained an understanding of what type of learning resources are available to you. All of this, however, needs to be put into practice, and even then, you are likely only doing the bare minimum. At the least, you're probably not standing out by a great margin. Is that what you have been working so hard for in the past, to be just like everybody else?

To truly get ahead – and stay there – you need to adopt key habits. Attending a training here and there will not cut it. A master of any field will tell you that it is habitual and deliberate practice that makes the difference.[15] Two simple yet powerful practices that can put you on the path toward excellence will be discussed next. If adopted, I guarantee that you will benefit both professionally and privately.

Reading Yourself to Success

Reading is crucial. As the old adage goes, *if you want to become a leader, you have to be a reader*. This holds true in consulting, too. The problem is that most people in full-time employment do not take the time to read, but you should know better. It should be in your own self-interest to read regularly and read more. After all, reading has palpable benefits, which help build a more bulletproof career in a knowledge society.

Regardless of whether you seek to become a star practitioner or just want to get by, here are five ways in which you personally benefit from reading.

> **1. Providing context:** If you want to be able to put things into context, you need to have a basic understanding of what's going on. Yes, I am referring to basic news here. You don't need to have all the answers, but at least have a general understanding of what is happening out there in the world. I know plenty of practitioners (both colleagues and competitors) who are nowhere near up to date, to put it mildly.
>
> Don't get me wrong: technical skills and industry expertise are important, and no news snippet is worth

forgoing expanding your knowledge in your own domain. However, without being able to see all of this in the bigger picture, none of it is going to matter.

Even the low-information diet proposed by Tim Ferriss[16] does not encourage complete abstinence from news. Instead, he argues in favor of a more deliberate, high-level approach to getting a basic understanding of what is going on. Being aware of current issues and being able to see connections are essential to understanding the world in which we live. Don't let your clients think you have been living under a rock.

2. **Broadening your horizons:** Expand your knowledge. Read material pertaining to your area of expertise, including current trends, new research, and whatever else can help sharpen your profile in your field. Particularly in the world of consulting, this is what clients expect, as they should.

Don't stop there! You should also read material that is completely unknown to you. Even better, read material that is completely unknown to both you and those with whom you compete. Chances are, you will get an invaluable edge just by being able to see new connections or to come up with original ideas.

3. **Challenging your own thinking:** Do not refrain from reading the opposite of what you might typically like. Read material with which you disagree. Tackle the confirmation bias of your newsfeed head-on.

The reason for this is simple: in order to be able to put yourself in someone else's shoes, a certain degree of mental openness is vital.

The problem is, as we grow up, we are meant to stand for something and are asked to have opinions. Choosing sides means favoring one over the other, which is not good for openness.

Openness, however, is essential in the modern world. Whether you work in multicultural teams or engage with different clients, you will eventually face challenges originating from different views of the world. Therefore, read (or at least skim through) the opposite of what you are normally interested in. If you think you will disagree with something, then you're missing the point. You are not meant to agree, simply to understand.

Being aware of potential differences is the first step. When you understand the other side, you can more easily accommodate and possibly turn around a situation in your own favor – with family, friends, colleagues, and, above all, clients.

4. **Kick-starting yourself:** In times of hardship or simply during the daily grind, a good read can provide strength for one's mind. In fact, it is likely one of the best things you can do to start off your day.

    It doesn't matter what you're into. For some, it is one of the holy books, while others prefer the latest self-help material. Another person might draw strength from philosophical classics (e.g., Seneca), and still others could find joy in reading autobiographies (e.g., Richard Branson's *Losing My Virginity*).

Whatever works for you is fine, but give yourself the gift of regular time to read. It can kick-start your day or provide answers when you need them most.

5. **Keeping your idea muscle working:** A recent study indicated a positive relationship between city size and the creativity of its population. However, rather than creativity increasing proportionally in a one-to-one manner, they found a consistent increase of greater than one to one (a superlinear scaling effect). "A city that was ten times larger than its neighbor wasn't ten times more innovative; it was seventeen times more innovative. A metropolis fifty times bigger than a town was 130 times more innovative."[17]

So what does this mean for you? As odd as this might sound, replicate a city for yourself. The more ideas you expose yourself to, the greater the creative benefit. While there are specific practices to enhance your fortitude in developing ideas (see the next section, "Becoming an Idea Machine"), it all starts with knowledge input.

The more diverse the topics, the better. They will activate your brain and enhance your creativity. Before you know it, your capacity to come up with ideas will skyrocket. Remember, ideas are what you are being paid for. Small ideas, big ideas . . . it doesn't matter. Just bring something new to the table!

In a nutshell, whatever you do, start reading more. Do it regularly, which means daily. Make it a habit to read thirty minutes each day if you can. Use any downtime that you may have, whether it is on the daily commute or while you're winding down after work. Don't become so immersed in your work that you forget about working on yourself. I know of many people who lacked the essential knowledge of current issues and had no idea about any new insights in their areas of expertise. Don't be like that. Being valuable means having ideas. To have ideas, you must expose yourself to new stuff – often. Scratch that; make it all the time.

There is value in reading, and no matter how great the demands on you at work, all of us should free up time to enhance our perspectives on the world. No one else will do it for you!

Becoming an Idea Machine

The second habit is to work toward becoming an idea machine. Regardless of what type of role you perform, most jobs no longer pay for mere execution. Proactivity is expected. That being said, being proactive is simple when you have a constant flow of ideas.

So, what is an idea machine? Someone who constantly comes up with ideas. No matter the situation, whether deliberately sought or not, these people are coming up with new concepts. Do all these ideas need to be groundbreaking? Of course not. With everything we practice, what we produce often makes no sense. Lots of ideas will be useless or even ridiculous. Don't limit your imagination by trying to exclusively come up with good ideas. Focus on quantity first. Quality will naturally follow.

The question is, how can you become a well of creativity? James Altucher wrote an in-depth post on how to become an idea machine.[18] Read it.

In essence, take a few minutes every day and come up with ten ideas for any topic. Again, these ideas do not have to be great. To come up with a topic, just ask yourself some question. Any question will do. It could be simple, complex, random, or directly aimed at solving a very concrete problem that you are currently facing. Here are some examples:

- What are ten ways to increase team morale on my current project?

- Which ten client prospects could benefit from the latest research conducted by my team?

- Which ten approaches could we take to attract high-caliber talent, in addition to my firm's existing recruiting activities?

- What are ten additional revenue streams my current client could tap into?

- What ten things have I learned today?

I take no credit for this approach, because it belongs to James Altucher. However, I highly believe in the concept. Anyone in a knowledge-based job should do the same; check out James's blog at www.jamesaltucher.com or order his book.[19]

Key Takeaways

♦ Acknowledge that continuous learning is not a buzzword. It is the very foundation to develop your consulting skills and expertise, and ultimately keeps you in business.

♦ Use all available internal resources. There are plenty of opportunities for junior consultants to cultivate knowledge, including classroom and online trainings, and knowledge-sharing platforms. It is up to you to make the most of these opportunities.

- Look elsewhere when internal resources are insufficient. Invest in books, online courses, and external courses to fill the identified learning gap. Try to secure funding from your firm.

- Take personal responsibility for your learning. Don't limit yourself to a standard curriculum. Develop an excessive reading habit to continuously broaden your horizons.

- Become an idea machine. Challenge yourself creatively. Come up with ten ideas every day to keep your brain well exercised.

CHAPTER 11
How to Build Your Network

"People do business with people they know and like."

Keith Ferrazzi, *Never Eat Alone*

Networking is a key activity in consulting. For junior consultants, establishing an internal network should be the first order of business. Every day consists of nurturing existing relationships and bonding with people you have not met yet.

First, I will give you my general take on networking. We will then look at how to network specifically as a junior consultant. We will continue with an illustration of five often-overlooked groups of people that many practitioners do not have on their radar, and highlight the importance of networking with them (Figure 10: Networking Landscape (optional)). We conclude the chapter with a deep dive into the mentor–mentee relationship, which may go well beyond your firm.

A Primer on Networking

Networking is the process of building relationships with other people. All parties should benefit from the relationship in some form or other. Benefits can take on many different shapes, from lending support and giving advice to opening doors. Connecting with other people is particularly important for junior practitioners trying to make themselves known in an organization. After all, if no one knows you, who is going to consider you for anything to begin with? Thus, you need to establish your network early on.

To be sure, networking does not primarily serve as a vehicle to solve problems. Reaching out to other people when you need their help might work every once in a while, but this is not technically networking. This is simply asking for help. Networking should not occur when you need help from other people; it should happen well before that.

Successful networkers rely on connections that they have nurtured for a long time before ever asking for anything in return. Seek to establish a connection first, and determine what you can bring to the relationship. How can you add value? How can you make the other person's life a little easier?

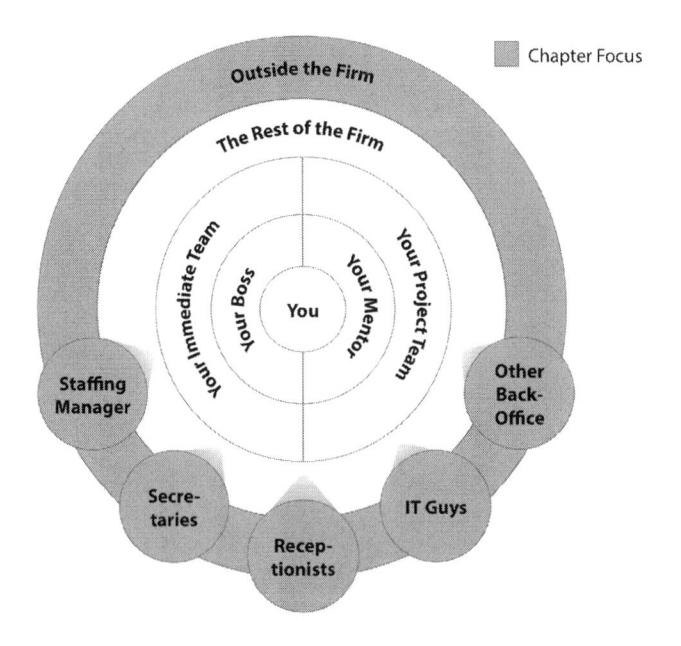

Figure 10: Networking Landscape (optional)

Effective Networking in Consulting

For aspiring consultants, it is vital to understand the importance of networking in consulting as well as potential pitfalls. At first, it may appear like an entirely different ball game from other professions, but to be sure, it does not have to be a daunting exercise.

The types of different stakeholders you are dealing with are manifold. Irrespective of the size of your company, you should never cut back on networking. Next, we will discuss how to network, what tools to use, where to network, and what to do in case there are limited networking opportunities.

How to Network

Follow the seven principles below to begin your networking activities on a solid foundation.

1. **Be likeable:** You should always come across as a genuinely nice person. Be humble, and do not try to impress by being too eager. Leave that to others. If anything, try to impress in a natural, modest fashion.

2. **Introduce yourself:** *Always* introduce yourself. If you meet someone you have not met yet, greet that person warmly. This is not just something to remember in your first weeks but should actually become your *modus operandi*. Regardless of whether people are more junior or senior to you, always connect. Understand who they are and where in the organization they fit.

   This also applies when you are working in an open-space office. You will frequently be surrounded by new faces, so don't become one of those guys who simply sneaks in and out, trying not to be seen. Trust me, they exist.

3. **Be goal-oriented:** When you network, try to have at least a vague idea of what you want to get out of the relationship as well as what you could bring to it. This will help you use your networking time more effectively. Instead of talking for hours on end with people who will have no impact on your professional development (e.g., if they work in an entirely different part of the organization), you will know when to stop after getting their names and professions. Be aware of what you should be looking for.

   Note: If you can learn something valuable from people in other parts of the organization, you should definitely tap into their knowledge. Some insights you gain from them or the connection itself might come in handy when you face future project challenges.

4. **Reach out frequently:** Given the relatively high turnover in the industry, you want to keep track of your network. Don't let farewell emails sent to "Corporate All" take you by surprise. If you have to, schedule follow-ups with specific people in your calendar. This is what the best networkers do. They don't take chances; they put the right systems in place.

5. **Follow up after first encounters:** We all meet a lot of people as we move through life. Often, we forget their names the minute after we have been introduced. Follow up the next day to stay on their minds.

6. **Take specific time to network:** You can network all day long, and then realize that you have not actually gotten much else done. Therefore, separate networking from formal working time.

7. **Don't gossip:** Many people have an interest in the office trash, but you never know what you might be getting yourself into. Thus, don't waste your time gossiping. Besides, if you're talking about other people, what do you expect them to do when you're not around?

If some of this sounds familiar, then you've been reading carefully. These principles partly take into account the objectives discussed in Chapter 2. In short, what works when you first start by and large will serve you well for the rest of your career.

Tools to Enhance Your Networking Activities

The best networkers do not leave things to chance. They have adopted systems or processes that enable them to network effectively. The following tools and practices are not exclusive, but they do give you a flavor of what can work.

1. **Calendar reminders (free):** One of the most effective practices is to regularly remind yourself to follow up with key people. In your calendar, you can schedule recurring events for a variety of reasons.

    - Calling your mentor (monthly)
    - Networking with peers (quarterly)
    - Reaching out to important groups of which you are a member (e.g., M&A affinity group, monthly/quarterly)
    - Birthdays (annually)

2. **Enhanced contacts in your email client (free):** The contact list in your email account can be further enhanced with additional information. You will have to do the work and enter the information yourself, but it might come in handy later.

3. **Nextcall app (Android; free):** Nextcall keeps track of how frequently you call certain people. Even better, you can cluster your contacts and assign different call intervals for each. An automatic reminder will then alert you when it is time to call a certain contact.

4. **Clinck app (iOS, Android; free):** Clinck allows you to easily share your contact details with people when you don't have your business cards handy.

5. **Excel-based relationship tracking (free):** One of the easiest ways to track key contacts is to set up a simple Excel tracking tool. You don't have to create these from scratch; search online for "Excel CRM template" for free resources to utilize.

6. **Evernote Business for Salesforce.com (paid):** While probably not required in your first two years, anyone working in a business driven by relationships should have Evernote Business on his or her radar. Salesforce.com is one of the most powerful customer relationship management (CRM) services. In combination with Evernote, the leading note-capturing application, these two form a powerful tool to deepen your professional relationships.

Where to Network

There are plenty of different networking opportunities available in consulting. While not exclusive to the industry, the nature of the project-, client-, or account-based work requires constant juggling of the workforce. This consequently makes people more apt to engage in networking opportunities. After all, everyone benefits!

When looking for networking opportunities, consider the following (timeless) options.

- **Office:** The office is a great networking playground. Particularly in open-space environments, you will meet plenty of people. Take advantage of that. Connect with those you know and introduce yourself to those you have not met yet.

- **Official events:** There will be regular events for your firm or part of the practice. Attend those unless there is a very good reason not to.

- **Email:** Reach out to connect. Email is particularly useful for those irregular updates when you are not sharing the same office.

- **Unofficial events:** There are no limits here. This could range from informal gatherings with your colleagues at a bar or breakfast before work to lunch meetings and brunch on the weekends.

There are those people who distinguish strictly between work and private matters. Let me be clear, you are not supposed to become "friends" with your entire firm. However, collaborative professional relationships will have to be nurtured just like personal relationships. They don't just happen; they require some effort. At the very least, regularly catching up over lunch or coffee is something you should consider.

What If There Are No Networking Opportunities?

There are *always* networking opportunities even though there are folks who claim that it was more difficult to build their networks than other professionals.

Typical Excuses

There may be situations that are less than ideal for working on your internal network. However, here is the good news: Most of this is due to excuses from those who will not last long. They likely include the following.

   1. **I Don't Have Time:** Everyone understands that project work is important. In fact, it is the most important thing

for you when you are first starting out. There will be periods when you will have no time for anything but your client deliverables. If you are lucky, your project is part of your practice. Therefore, you will likely stay "close to home," where maintaining a constant level of exchange will be easier.

However, you might be assigned to a project that does not belong to your practice or that is very remote. Even then, no one will accept complete silence. In fact, the exact opposite is the case. If you find yourself detached from the rest of the group, there will be an expectation for you to proactively reach out. Not having time is not an excuse. There is always time for a short note to one's team.

2. **It's Just Not Common Over Here:** Others claim that some environments are not right for networking. Apart from the office, opportunities to connect may actually be quite rare. Perhaps it has just never been done in a specific team or practice.

What does this tell you about your team? More importantly, what does this mean for you? Basically, you will have a great opportunity to stand out if you can set things in motion. People in consulting are supposed to be self-starters. No one will stop you from doing something worthwhile for the team.

How to Maximize Poor Networking Opportunities

There are always ways to work around difficult situations. What clients pay us for will work for you, too: being creative and proactive. Use the following ideas as starting points to create networking opportunities and make yourself known.

- **Dial in to team calls:** At some point, you might realize that the direct benefits are minimal, but early in your career, you have no reason not to join team calls. You would be surprised how many people never make an effort to attend. Eventually, these are the same guys who are unknown in the firm or practice, if they are known for anything at all (only slightly exaggerating here).

- **Schedule team drinks:** Talk to your boss and ask him or her if you could invite the team out for team drinks. Your boss will probably appreciate your initiative and make some of the budget available. These types of activities also tend to go a long way in performance ratings.

- **Send your team an update when abroad:** At times, you might end up on a project that is truly out of sight and possibly out of mind. Perhaps you are required to work on a client site all week. In such cases, meeting in person (and perhaps attending calls) may be a challenge. You should at least occasionally notify your team that you're still alive.

  Also, follow up with your team lead and managers one month before your scheduled project roll-off. Don't disappear from their radars. By sending a quick update, you will stand out despite being out of sight. As with anything, don't overdo it.

- **Share useful information with the team:** Apart from sending an update to your team (especially to senior leaders), you might want to consider sharing material or information that you deem relevant and useful to others. This could be anything, including new tools or the latest research in your field.

What else can you think of? Don't limit your options to these suggestions!

So far, we have covered Networking 101 in consulting. Now, let's take a closer look at how to network with specific people in consulting firms. This is in addition to those stakeholders we discussed in Chapter 4. Here, we will elucidate important stakeholders that many people do not consider to be part of their network.

Often-Overlooked People to Connect With

All the networking advice in the world will only get you so far if you forget to see the bigger picture. Time and again, I have seen people struggle to build their networks because they were too narrowly focused. I was certainly not a natural-born networker myself. I had to learn a fair share in my early years, too.

What some people never get right is looking beyond their group of ordinary practitioners. Some are so focused on their immediate environment that they fail to see other important pieces of the jigsaw puzzle that can make or break their progress in consulting. For simplicity's sake, let's call these people "gatekeepers." They are individuals who, on paper, may not play a crucial role in the organization but can stand in your way by their sole existence or open doors for you that you were completely unaware of.

Again, if you are working in a small practice, it is very likely that not all of the below roles will apply to your situation. Nevertheless, the tasks performed by the five groups below are very common. Thus, even in small firms, someone will be responsible for these tasks, and therefore will qualify as a valuable networking target.

What follows is a brief introduction of each of these five groups: staffing managers, secretaries, receptionists, IT guys, and other back-office staff. For each group, we will discuss their relevance, their most common challenges, and ways to develop and maintain mutually beneficial relationships with them.

Staffing Managers

Staffing managers are in charge of allocating staff. Whether it is regarding client engagements or internal work, wherever there is a resource need, staffing managers try to match requirements with available resources. You will usually find designated roles such as this in larger firms.

Why They Matter

Staffing managers fulfill an indispensable role in project-based work environments. Projects can start and finish at any time. Thus, resource planning is crucial. The better your staffing manager is doing this, the happier the leadership team will be.

Why should this matter to you? If you can build a good relationship with your staffing manager, you may benefit in at least two ways. Your staffing manager can 1) put you on projects in which you may have an interest or 2) temporarily save you from being assigned to less than ideal pieces of work.

Their Challenges

Since staffing managers are not involved in the day-to-day work of practitioners, they face a number of challenges.

First, they do not know which projects will go ahead, be put on hold, scaled down, etc. In order to do the job well, they have to rely on information provided by partners, project managers, and ordinary practitioners.

Second, staffing managers have the daunting task of matching available project roles with free resources. Resource availability should be straightforward, but often is not.

People that appear to be available will suddenly get blocked by senior people, be unreachable, or become surprisingly unavailable. All of this can and should be avoided in the interest of the firm through accurate availability updates from practitioners. Staffing managers can conduct quality checks of data submission accuracy, which may help to penalize extreme offenders. At the end of the day, however, they will have to work with the data they receive.

How to Keep Them Happy

There are a few actions that will ensure you are off to a good start with your staffing manager. In the beginning, catch up with him or her in person. Have lunch or coffee, introduce yourself, and mention your interests as well as whatever you deem relevant for your career.

Going forward, do your homework. If you are asked to regularly update your availability forecast, then you should absolutely do so. I recommend that you schedule recurring weekly reminders in your calendar (e.g., Monday @ 8:00 a.m., unless there is some specific submission deadline) for you to confirm that your update is still accurate.

It is also good practice to contact the staffing manager, while remembering to cc your boss, one month before your expected project roll-off. This allows them to find new opportunities for you.

In addition, regularly catch up with your staffing manager either in person, by phone, or via email. Tell him or her about your situation and planned activities (e.g., potential project extension, holidays). Unsolicited updates show that you are proactive and are taking your staffing manager's needs into account.

Secretaries

Secretaries are not always known by that name. Chances are, they will be called an "executive assistant" or something similar to that. That also indicates their current role. First and foremost, these individuals support a partner. Thus, do not expect them to be overly proactive in seeking to support you or other (senior) practitioners.

Why They Matter

Secretaries are the senior leaders' guardians. They are the primary gatekeeper between you and your boss. They manage the agenda and often perform an initial review of the inbox, distinguishing the important from the unimportant.

As a result, they are the ones who can squeeze you into a tight schedule. It might only be five minutes, but that's often all it takes to get a yes/no from your boss. Secretaries can open doors – or keep them shut.

Their Challenges

Given the people they work for, their workload can often be intense. At times, practitioners in consulting tend to forget this. Also, a lot of people will be asking for something from them. To be more precise, they want something *through* them, as those "secretaries" are standing in between practitioners and their boss.

For the most part, secretaries do a tremendous job without getting much back in return. They might get a bit of courtesy from the senior leaders, but that's about it. Moreover, there are no clear career paths for them besides staying close to their senior leaders. This can be frustrating for those more junior in their role.

How to Keep Them Happy

Obviously, as a junior practitioner, there is not much you can do about the work of secretaries and the challenges they face. However, you can give them some sincere attention when you're around. Don't only pass by when you need something or have a request. Be considerate and stop to have a genuine chat. Make them feel that you are part of the same team and respect them.

Receptionists

Guess what? Receptionists do have their own place. It's called the reception. Not too surprising...

Why They Matter

Receptionists are important both at your office and on a client site. Granted, they primarily provide logistical support (e.g., making meeting rooms available, providing access to external visitors, calling taxis, etc.), but this role should not be understated. In your day-to-day activities, it will make a huge difference whether you have friendly support from the receptionists when you are in need or instead have to beg for their time. Make an effort to bond with receptionists.

Their Challenges

Receptionists meet a lot of people on any given day, but how many of those actually make an effort to exchange more than a simple greeting?

Also, keep in mind that they have barely any of the perks ordinary practitioners enjoy. Fancy dinners? Team events? Weekly company drinks? Receptionists are usually left out of the equation unless it is a firm-wide annual event.

In short, receptionists seldom receive the recognition they deserve. Time and again, junior practitioners in particular make the mistake of perceiving and (even worse!) treating receptionists as colleagues of a lower rank. This might not be suicide for your career, but it can still have negative consequences.

How to Keep Them Happy

To keep receptionists happy and build friendly relationships with them, stop doing what everyone else does. Instead, talk to them regularly and show some interest. Don't only interact with them when you have requests. Everyone does that, but you should know better.

IT Guys

Your IT department takes care of all the technical equipment that practitioners use on a daily basis, whether remotely or at the office. They regularly update, refurbish, restock, and resolve technical issues when necessary.

Why They Matter

One of the first groups you will probably meet early in your career are the guys in IT, either because they hand out your new devices or because something you need simply doesn't work. However, they will be instrumental to you far beyond your first days on the job.

Every now and then, you will experience hiccups with your technology. For example, you might have trouble connecting to a client's network due to security settings, or some specific piece of software will have to be bought for your project purposes. Whatever the situation may be, where your equipment is involved, your IT department will have to be consulted. It therefore pays to have (very) good relationships with them. Otherwise, you might be told to open a ticket and wait . . .

Their Challenges

Just like many other back-office roles, the guys in IT suffer from a low level of recognition. For the most part, they are problem solvers (but few people actually thank them), and they are commonly scolded when their turnaround time is not quick enough.

How to Keep Them Happy

IT guys are easy to please, given the low level of recognition they usually receive from the firm. A chat over coffee and showing genuine interest in how things are going for them will go a long way to establishing better (*read*: more personal) relationships than most practitioners have with IT professionals.

If you want to go above and beyond, do what successful senior people do and treat the IT guys to some considerate, but relatively effortless, courtesies during the holiday season (e.g., chocolates).

Other Back-Office Support Staff

The back-office support staff includes professions like marketing, human resources, recruiting, finance, legal, or research. They differ from the previous four groups in that they are "optional" from a networking perspective. Their value can be significant if you engage them properly. However, if you do not, it will probably not impact your career negatively either. In contrast, you can hardly get anything done if you are not properly handling your networking with the first four groups.

Why They Matter

The benefits you can draw from these other support functions are manifold. At the core, however, their importance boils down to greater flexibility. If you have them on your side . . .

- Marketing can help you publish your study and even advise on how to secure funding

- HR may speed up the recruiting process with a candidate that you have preselected for your team

- Legal may provide counsel, despite being knee-deep in their own issues

- Finance may process certain invoices on your behalf or provide payment extensions

- Research may open up their network and provide you with contacts you could not have personally secured

Their Challenges

In support functions, a different pace exists than in a typical consulting practice. Therefore, it does not go over well if you approach them with ad hoc requests that they could not have anticipated. Likewise, only showing up when you need something from them is not a good way to nurture the relationship. Due to this fact, support functions might not always come across as the most proactive.

Besides, by the very nature of their work, support functions are rarely involved in most of the "fun stuff" at work. There might be firm-wide Christmas parties and summer events, but how often do they take place? Not often.

How to Keep Them Happy

Given the relatively low level of recognition they receive on a daily basis, you don't have to move mountains in order to keep them happy. They appreciate feeling like a part of the wider firm, so go ahead and invite them to whatever firm-wide occasion you can think of. Informal after-work drinks don't need to be limited to other consultants.

Besides, treat them like you would want others to treat you. You like to be greeted, so greet them. Don't miss the opportunity to briefly, casually connect with them when meeting in the hallway, elevator, or passing by their offices. Listen in on their views, worries, and suggestions. It will pay off handsomely if you can build sincere trusting relationships.

Having learned why and how to successfully connect with internal, often-overlooked stakeholders, let's look in detail at one of the most important aspects of your career: the mentor–mentee relationship.

A View on Mentors

Mentors are very important. They can make the difference between getting ahead in your career and staying put.

In your firm, a senior practitioner will likely be assigned to act as your mentor. We call him or her the internal mentor. This can be a match made in heaven or turn out to be a complete disaster. To help you determine which situation you're in, we will first look at a profile of a good internal mentor. I will then describe what to do in case you wish to change your internal mentor.

As it is also good practice to have a trusted advisor outside your organization, we will conclude this section by discussing the rationale for having an external mentor and explaining where to find one.

What Is a Good Internal Mentor?

The profile of a good internal mentor is quite straightforward. Obviously, character traits are different, and what appeals to me might not appeal to you. The mentor–mentee relationship is very personal, so you should ensure that you click with the person giving you career advice and guidance.

Nevertheless, there are certain competencies that a good internal mentor should have to be truly valuable in your career progression:

- Minimum four years of experience with the firm

- Started off as a junior practitioner in the firm (i.e., knows exactly what the challenges for juniors are)

- Was promoted according to plan or faster (i.e., knows how to get ahead)

- Willing to give honest feedback

- Sports an extensive internal network, which may be leveraged for a mentee's cause

- Diligently performs mentoring duties by making time available, when need be, and holding mentees accountable

Note: All of the above is informed by my very positive mentee experience (hat tip to Marco Issenmann and Felix Hauber), as well as the less than ideal experiences of some colleagues of mine.

What to Do If You Want a New Internal Mentor

At times, you and your internal mentor might not be a perfect match. In that case, there are always ways to change and find a new one. Here are the four steps to accomplish that.

1. **Do not speak to your mentor immediately:** Those more senior to you usually have more experience and boast a wider network in the firm. Therefore, you want to proceed strategically (*read*: carefully). You want to avoid ruining your relationship with your mentor and potentially shutting alternative doors from the start.

2. **Understand the official process:** Contact HR or ask fellow colleagues you trust about how the process of changing one's mentor typically works in your firm.

3. **Identify a potential new mentor:** Identify a potential mentor, and ask if he or she would be available and willing to take you on as a new mentee in the future.

You do not have to be overly specific about your current mentor or the fact that you are considering making a change. Keep it informal and say that you think you might benefit from a fresh perspective.

4. **Follow the official process:** Once you have found someone who generally agrees to mentor you, have a word with your existing mentor. Let him or her know that you plan to proceed with the next official steps.

To summarize, it's essential to have a great relationship with your mentor. As such, I recommend that you first make an effort to improve the relationship in case it is not working to your satisfaction. Only after you have tried to improve it (and have spoken with your mentor on how to turn things around) should you go ahead and seek alternatives.

The Benefits of an External Mentor

Internal mentors are not the only source of guidance. In fact, everyone should have an external mentor in addition to the one assigned by one's firm.

An external mentor can benefit your development in ways that an internal mentor probably cannot. For starters, an external mentor is objective. Clearly, someone outside the firm does not have any say in your career progression within the firm, but that is also the biggest advantage. He or she is not related to your firm and can provide you with a perspective that internal colleagues cannot. In addition, you can freely share your concerns and career aspirations (which may go beyond your firm) without worrying about negative consequences.

Finding an External Mentor

There is not a single best approach for finding an external mentor. One thing is certain; you'll have to invest both effort and time. You can't find a mentor overnight.

To get you thinking, start considering any of the following people to act as a future external mentor:

- A university professor you have always admired

- A relative you respect for his or her business acumen

- Someone in your local community who has had ten to twenty years of experience in his or her field

Focus on people who have enjoyed success in some form or other, and whose advice you genuinely respect.

How to Connect with Your Mentor

Whether you have an internal or external mentor, or both, you should seek to create a mutually beneficial relationship. As such, this should not be a one-way exchange of ideas and rewards. Your mentor invests time in your development, so you should reciprocate in some form or other. To enhance the relationship do the following.

- **Provide frequent updates:** Your mentor should always have a clear idea about your current situation. This does not mean you have to report weekly but catching up once a month (or quarterly at the very least) helps keep your mentor in the loop. You should also inform him or her as soon as you encounter challenges that may have an impact on your professional development. Critical turning points should not take your mentor by surprise.

- **Acknowledge feedback:** You do not have to agree with all the feedback you receive, but it is good practice to thoroughly consider certain advice and inform your mentor on specific steps taken and progress made.

- **Show gratitude:** A simple thank you never hurts, but that's probably not enough to build a truly great relationship. Instead, express your gratitude by taking your mentor out for lunch or dinner, buy him or her a bottle of wine, or simply write him or her a little thank you note.

Key Takeaways

- Build your network to advance your career. This cannot be accomplished overnight. It requires time and effort. Put systems in place to regularly nurture relationships to simplify this process.

- Give first. Invest in your relationships. Seek to provide value to your network before asking for anything in return.

- Attend networking events. Do not forgo opportunities to connect with fellow colleagues. Initiate these opportunities if they're lacking in your firm.

- Network with those who are left out. Engage in collaborative relationships with back-office support staff. This is an inexpensive way to really get things done, along with being the right thing to do.

- Invest in building a strong mentor–mentee relationship. Consider having both internal and external mentors to benefit from direct career support and objective council, respectively. Don't be afraid to change mentors, if necessary.

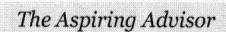

CHAPTER 12

Using Downtime to Your Advantage

> "The only times I'm not relaxed are when I haven't got a project on the go."
>
> **Iain Sinclair**

Consultants are paid to help clients get better, so sitting idle in the office is not part of the game plan. Accordingly, your seniors will try to staff you as quickly as possible and turn you from a cost into a revenue generator. In other words, you should be on a project most of the time.

However, there will be moments when this is not the case. In fact, you might be stuck at the office for an indefinite period of time. Whether you call it being on the beach, on the bench, or simply downtime, this chapter tries to break down how to make the most of it.

First, I will explain the typical work performed when one is not on a project. Following that, we will look at what actions to take when one is completely new to the firm and then when one is slightly more experienced.

There Is Always Something to Do

Many consultants find being at the office more intense than performing actual external client work. Clearly, this differs between firms and even between individual teams. When not being staffed, consultants usually support the following.

- **Business development (BD):** Business development stands for all those activities performed to generate additional business, either directly or indirectly. As such, these may include proposal work, research, marketing activities, etc.

- **Practice development (PD):** Practice development builds, manages, or maintains the consulting practice. It is not business-driven, but follows an entirely internal rationale. Activities are manifold and include event organization, internal process improvement, newsletters, charity work, etc.

- **Talent:** Talent work seeks to enhance the firm's human resources. Activities include recruiting support and giving (or helping to organize) trainings.

When Just Starting Out

The key action items for you to focus on when you are starting out have already been discussed. Again, do not expect to be staffed on a project immediately.

Instead, focus on the key points from Chapter 3. If you have accomplished all of those steps, then you should engage in some serious networking. Offer your help wherever you can. Eventually, your value will shine through and you will be offered project opportunities. Refer to Chapter 4, and Chapter 11 for further guidance.

When Not on a Project Despite Prior Experience

When you have been with your firm for some time, you will have gained a certain amount of practical experience. Accordingly, there should always be some type of demand for you.

However, every now and then, you will still experience downtime. Oftentimes, this will merely be a few days between two projects. That's nothing to worry about. You should try to recharge your batteries during that period. (*Note*: A good mentor will advise you to do this, while your partner will not, for obvious reasons.)

Let us now look at likely reasons for you being off a project, as well as specific steps to get you back into the action.

Why You Might Not Be on a Project

Occasionally, you might experience a more extended period of time off a project. There are many possible reasons for this. The most common ones are listed below.

> 1. **Lack of projects:** In case the project pipeline has dried up, it will be difficult to staff you, for obvious reasons. However, that does not mean that you should sit idle. In fact, I would argue that there should be plenty to do in such a situation: business development, filing reference material for future use, doing research, etc.
>
> 2. **You are blocked:** At times, some senior colleague might have requested to staff you on an upcoming opportunity. Others may not invite you onto their projects unless that senior person agrees. While it is good to be in demand by several people, don't get caught in between. Also, don't let yourself be blocked indefinitely. You would not be the first one to wait forever for a project that is always "about to kick off" but eventually never materializes.

3. **You are lacking the skills:** This is the worst situation but also not the end of the world. An honest discussion with your mentor, staffing manager, or boss can do wonders here. Be honest about your own capabilities and ask for guidance on how to improve. Additional pointers can be found in Chapter 10.

With these root causes for being on the bench in mind, let's focus on what you should do to shorten your downtime and get the most out of it while it lasts.

Shorten Downtime Between Projects

Managing your time off a project actually starts before you find yourself in this situation. The following five actions, especially Action 1, should be considered while you are still on a project. Also, keep in mind that there is always something that needs to be done in consulting firms. In other words, real downtime shouldn't exist. However, if you're lucky and can freely choose where to direct your attention, take Actions 2–5 as pointers to get you started.

Action 1: Manage your roll-off

Even if you are on a project, you should start thinking about your roll-off. Do this well in advance, as you might be aware of your project end date. Most likely, the rest of the firm is not. Don't let this take them by surprise when you suddenly reappear at the office. Provide sufficient information beforehand, so both your boss and staffing manager can think of upcoming opportunities that will benefit you, the firm, and them.

Action 2: Control communication

As will be explained in more detail in Chapter 15 (in the section titled, "Example IV: Sudden Project Roll-Off"), controlling communication when rolling off a project is critical. There should be consistent communication, regardless of whether your project termination was planned or occurred by surprise. Aligning with your mentor is good practice for this. You want to avoid a situation where your status as being off-project takes on a life of its own, as it might in organizations where people talk a lot.

Action 3: Work your network

Be proactive. Don't come back to the office and wait for others to approach you. Go out hunting for interesting opportunities. However, always ensure that you are fully aligned with your boss. Don't commit to support anything or anyone without informing your boss. He or she is the one paying you, and chances are, there may already be other plans for you.

Action 4: Learn

When you're not on a project and not being drawn into late-night proposal work, use your time wisely and commit yourself to engaging in learning opportunities. Sign up for courses, both e-learning and in classroom environments, and make an investment in your own career. This is your chance to build up expertise in your area. Dig deep! Learn key concepts, find out about the latest research, and delve into nitty-gritty industry details. For more specific pointers, refer to Chapter 10.

Action 5: Take a vacation

If it's somewhat convenient for you (and family or friends), consider taking a vacation after rolling off a project. It is infinitely easier to go on holiday when you're not staffed than when you are in the midst of a project, even if you mention your potential plans up front.

Unless other emergencies require everyone's attention, your boss will likely be open to you taking time off. Maybe it is just a week or a couple of days, but be sure to take advantage of your holidays. Don't forgo vacation days to which you are legally entitled. No one benefits from you not taking a break – neither the firm, nor yourself.

Key Takeaways

- Expect downtime between projects. Be patient and focus on building your network if you are just starting out. Thoroughly reflect on potential reasons for your downtime (e.g., lack of projects, blocked for potential future opportunities, or lack of skills) if you have been with the firm for a while.

- Communicate your project roll-off early to minimize downtime. Reach out to your network, including your staffing manager, ideally one month before being back at the office.

- Take advantage of downtime. If you find yourself off a project, engage in learning opportunities or take a vacation.

CHAPTER 13
How to Get Measured Well

> "Don't mistake activity with achievement."
>
> **John Wooden**

CONSULTING IS VERY FEEDBACK-DRIVEN compared to other industries. Regardless of the size of the firm, regular assessments of your work will occur. This is also the case when you're not in a typical up-or-out environment.

This chapter sheds light on the most pressing issues when faced with performance management from the perspective of a junior consultant. It is also informed by experiencing firsthand how many people are unable to accept constructive feedback – even though they should.

We will first look at why performance management matters. Second, we shall discuss the steps in a typical performance year. Finally, I will provide some pointers about mitigating some of the most common challenges and how to receive feedback in the best way possible.

Why Performance Management Matters

Performance management is crucial in the consulting field, but clearly, there are caveats. You will probably experience situations that seem unfair. Effort that you make might not always translate directly into equal rewards. In fact, most people feel that they never get paid enough. That's just the way it is.

However, given that you've made it this far in the book, you're likely one of those people who the industry is always looking for: ambitious, motivated, willing to learn, and possessed of personal drive. Therefore, you should not be overly concerned about performance management; in fact, you'll probably appreciate the process.

Helping You Develop Yourself

First and foremost, performance management will help you in your own development by holding you accountable and pointing you toward areas to focus on in the future.

At the beginning of each performance year, you will define certain objectives. These are focal areas that you want to pay attention to during the upcoming performance cycle. While you are being observed in the context of your current level's expectations, objectives can be very personal. Depending on your strengths, weaknesses, and motivation, you will agree with your mentor on which things to focus on and what "success" at the end of the year would look like.

Performance discussions at the end of the year will then be used to measure your progression against your objectives. Your final rating and accompanying feedback will form the foundation in defining your new objectives for the following performance cycle. Thus, performance management can be a vital and ongoing system that helps you address weak points and become measurably better over time.

When I started out, Excel-based analytical skills were one of my development areas. I could get by, but like many others, I would not have regarded myself as "above average" either. As a result, one of my key objectives remained "enhancing Excel-based analytical skills" for a number of years. Therefore, I sought out opportunities (*read*: projects, business development, and internal research activities) that would allow me to test the waters a bit more. Also, the feedback I requested was always related to my analytical performance.

Clearing out the Bad Guys

Effective performance management can also be a useful tool to identify low performers in the organization. Essentially, this will enable two things.

First, it will allow the firm to put those who are currently struggling on a new track. Specific feedback and an action plan for low performers can turn them around to become valuable assets for the firm. After all, training someone new all over again is much more time-consuming (*read*: costs more money) than nudging someone back on track.

If all of this fails, obviously, performance management should not refrain from dismissing low performers. It is in the interest of the firm and each practitioner working with the low performer, because the morale of others will fall when they realize that slack in the system is not being dealt with.

The Performance Management Process

The very structure of the performance management process differs between firms. Also, remember that performance ratings are made either annually or biannually. For the sake of explanation, let's assume that we're dealing with an annual process, in which case, it will look as follows (see Figure 11: Sample Performance Management Process).

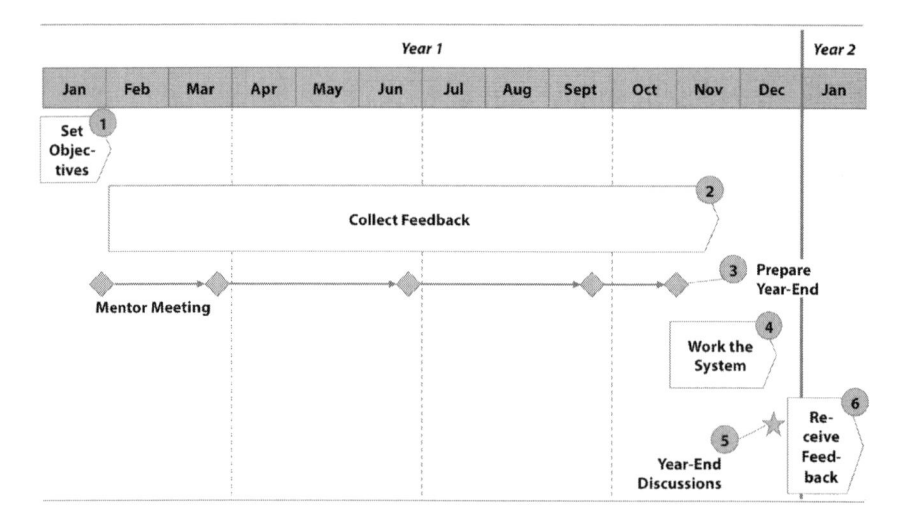

Figure 11: Sample Performance Management Process

1. **Months 0–1, define performance objectives:** At the beginning of each performance year (which may or may not coincide with the financial year), you will agree on SMART[20] objectives with your mentor.

2. **Months 1–11, collect feedback (ongoing):** Throughout the year, you will collect feedback on your work. This includes both client work and internal activities. The key here is to request specific feedback that can somehow be tied back to your original performance objectives.

3. **Month 11, prepare year-end discussion:** Toward the end of the performance year, you will meet with your mentor again. (*Note*: You should have regular contact

with your mentor throughout the year.) This discussion primarily serves to provide your mentor with a concise, firsthand account of your performance so that he or she can represent you best in front of the senior leadership (see Point 5).

You will likely agree on a short action plan, including requesting outstanding feedback and confirmations, completing certain mandatory trainings, and ticking other boxes that your company may require (e.g., legal obligations, holiday take-over approval).

4. **Months 11–12, work the system:** You and your mentor will execute the plan on which you both agreed. This means that your mentor works his or her network and reaches out to key people whose support is needed during performance rating discussions. Here, you may think of those (senior) people with whom you worked during the performance year as well as your boss and, at times, clients. This will serve to garner support and validate specific feedback, while also helping to mitigate certain risks (e.g., when you have received any poor feedback).

   Meanwhile, you will complete all open items that you and your mentor identified earlier (e.g., collecting feedback and complying with firm-wide requirements).

   In addition, you might draft a one- or two-page overview of your performance as a cheat sheet for your mentor. This typically includes projects worked on, utilization number (i.e., percentage of project work), key feedback, trainings attended, and other activities (including vacations, if any).

Note: Reaching out to key people just prior to year-end discussions will likely backfire. You and your mentor should maintain relationships with those individuals that have a say in your development throughout the year.

5. **Month 12, discuss performance and agree on final ratings:** During the final performance discussions, your mentor will present on your behalf. These sessions are typically held separately for each level.

Usually, the ultimate objective is to squeeze the range of practitioners into a bell curve. Thus, there can only be a handful of overachievers. The vast majority will be rated at a similar level.

Each practitioner will be represented by his or her mentor (often for less than two minutes). This brief presentation should conclude with a rating suggestion to the panel. This is best accomplished when other practitioners have already been discussed, as your mentor will be able to put things (and your particular case) into context.

Note: Your mentor should not be the first to speak, regardless of how busy he or she may be that day. Otherwise, you will end up as the benchmark, and, through a process similar to horse-trading, slowly see your rating drop over the course of the session.

While most ratings will have been agreed upon after the session, there might be some borderline cases. Those will be discussed and resolved in the following days.

6. **Month 12+, receive rating and feedback, and conclude performance year:** Just before the start of the new performance year, you will receive your year-end rating and corresponding feedback. Depending on the depth of the latter, this might directly affect the new objectives you set for yourself.

Performance Management Challenges

Now, let me share a more personal view. The reason I had for writing this guide was not to provide a generic overview that you could have gotten from your HR department. Instead, this chapter, like the rest of the book, is intended to help you understand how things usually work and teach you specific steps to navigate the consulting world in the best way possible.

A chapter on performance management would not be complete without addressing some of the recurring criticisms and potential remedies. By and large, the key reason for people criticizing performance ratings is due to their lack of transparency. Regardless of what senior practitioners might say, the process is usually not very transparent. Knowing how the process works is not the same as having insight into the actual dealings and understanding what has been negotiated in year-end discussions. This is where most of the criticism stems from. Ratings and the rationale thereof are not publicly announced, which leaves room for speculation.

One frequent perception is that ratings are not fair, slightly biased, and highly dependent on having viable connections within the network. In my opinion, the only way to address such criticism is to provide full openness. At the very least, ratings and corresponding feedback should be visible for each and every person. However, I am realistic enough to know that such changes are unlikely to be made in most organizations, so consider the following criteria that affect your year-end rating and work to improve them going forward.

Your Quality of Work

The Problem

I am convinced that the most important criterion for your rating remains the quality of your work. If you do a good job, then you will be off to a good start in the performance discussion. However, keep in mind, doing a good job is expected. Delivering on expectations usually does not get you very far. On the other hand, if you fail to deliver, this will hit you hard.

The Remedy

In order to truly stand out, your work has to be exceptional. Not once, but *consistently*. Certain pieces of work tend to stand out more than others, so you will need to be somewhat selective in what jobs you pick up. Thus, seek out great opportunities to learn from, continuously strive to become better, and consistently deliver high-quality work.

Your Visibility

The Problem

Apart from good work, you will have to ensure that people immediately know who is being discussed when they hear your name. You do not have to run naked down the hallway, screaming your name, but you should be known in some form or other. This is particularly important if you happen to be working on a remote project, which makes establishing/maintaining an office presence difficult.

The Remedy

Do not assume that people will happen to know you somehow. People won't know you unless you take matters into your own hands. Visibility is something that should be dealt with from Day 1, as it takes time to establish. The best way to enhance your visibility is to volunteer for high-profile tasks and achieve them with exceptional quality. Such tasks include all those whose outcomes are widely shared within the firm (or your particular part of it) and should ideally come with personal acknowledgement.

Moreover, in everything you do, be your own marketer. No one will provide free publicity for you. You have to take care of it yourself. If you don't, you're missing out. Research shows that actual performance doesn't always matter as much as being able to create favorable impressions.[21] Thus, follow this basic sequence: tell others what you will do, do it, and then showcase what you've done. However, make sure that you actually deliver on your promises. Too many people make lots of noise without actually following through and this will definitely hurt them down the road.

Finally, you have to make an effort to work the system yourself prior to year-end discussions. You want to ensure that you are on the radars of key decision makers all year long. Communicate your own view of the year and realistic rating expectations. This does not have to be too specific (i.e., a specific number isn't required), but if you want to get promoted, people should know why after having met you.

Sure enough, this should be a yearlong exercise. Don't start courting seniors two weeks before the rating sessions. This will reflect negatively on you, as you are clearly trying to win them over at the last minute.

People You Have Worked With

The Problem

Depending on the size of your firm, you will eventually run the risk of supporting the "wrong" part of it. In larger organizations, year-end performance discussions are held within subgroups, meaning that performance discussions do not always include the firm's entire leadership. You and your mentor might find limited support for your case simply because of the firm's organizational structure.

In one memorable year, I worked on a number of projects that I fully enjoyed and from which I learned a great deal. However, at year-end, I realized that my peers were in a somewhat better starting position for the final ratings. This was not due to significantly better feedback, but rather because I had supported people from another part of the firm who had no say in my year-end discussion. My peers had their project leads sitting right in their performance discussions. You can probably guess who had a slight edge.

The Remedy

The remedy is simple: Seek out projects close to home. These do not necessarily have to be with your own team, but the people you will be working for should play at least some role in your final year-end discussion. Obviously, you will have limited say about which projects to support when you start, but try to avoid being staffed on (long-term) projects away from your part of the firm.

Little Project Feedback

The Problem

Quality feedback is valuable and having a lot is much better than having little. It is therefore important to have an adequate amount of feedback in any given performance year.

As a general rule, a junior practitioner should not stay on the same project (or with the same client) for more than six months in the first two years. You will learn so much more from being exposed to different client environments and project teams than you ever could when staying with one project for an extended period. It will not only benefit you from a learning perspective, but will also help to build your internal network within the firm. Unfortunately, the reality is sometimes different. As staffing people on long-term projects is convenient, you might not be exposed to sufficient learning environments and might not have the opportunity to request various examples of feedback, which is important for year-end ratings.

The Remedy

For whatever pieces of work you deliver, ask for feedback. Whether this is internal or external work, mention early that you need feedback and schedule this to ensure that it gets done.

If you find yourself being staffed for too long on a single thing, speak to your mentor first and with your boss second, if at all. Also, do not speak with your project manager. He or she has no interest in letting you off the project unless you have been underperforming.

Poor Mentor

The Problem

Your mentor is a crucial player in your performance rating. His or her role starts well before the actual year-end discussion. First of all, your mentor will have to know how to succeed in the firm. For this, you want to have useful and realistic performance objectives. Typically, these are referred to as SMART objectives and should combine personal interests, grade-level performance expectations, and firm objectives. Your mentor should be aware of the intricacies of setting and achieving one's objectives and should guide you in defining them up front. In addition, your mentor will have to ensure that you remain on track throughout the year and, as such, hold you accountable.

Finally, you will not be permitted to present your own case in the year-end discussion. Your mentor will participate on your behalf. If you are unlucky, your mentor will not be properly prepared (e.g., not work the system prior to the session), lack experience (e.g., introducing you first or suggesting unrealistic ratings), show poor engagement (e.g., not actively participate in the discussion), have no internal network to build upon, or even forget the date of your year-end discussion.

The Remedy

Pick the right mentor. Apart from being able to work together with your mentor, you need to ensure that he or she can actually provide appropriate support. A good mentor will have several years of experience in the firm and a successful track record of past mentor–mentee relationships. To find such a mentor, you will have to ask around. I recommend opting for those who started as juniors in your firm themselves, as they will have the best understanding of what works and what does not.

If you are assigned to a mentor who is new to the firm, run! Unless he or she is the new star of the firm (unlikely), consider changing your mentor no later than six months into the performance year. For more details on how to change your mentor, see Chapter 11.

These are just some of the potential pitfalls in performance management. Some of these challenges may be more relevant when working in larger organizations. Nonetheless, it helps to be aware of these potential traps and take precautionary action.

How to Receive Feedback

Let's shift our focus to the feedback you receive throughout the year. First, I will provide some general thoughts about feedback in the consulting field, and then I will explain how to best deal with both negative and positive feedback.

The Nature of Feedback

There are many different types of feedback in consulting. It can be very extensive in written form, via a central reporting system, or just a short conversation at the water cooler. As such, there is no specific guidance on how often you should seek feedback. To be sure, every major work you complete should be supported with specific feedback on your performance. As a rule of thumb, consider anything for which you invested more than twenty hours to require feedback.

Keep in mind, though, that feedback is very personal. Thus, a lot comes down to individual perception. If you do not click with someone immediately, you may want to seek ways to improve the situation. If you realize only afterward, then learn your lesson. Identify ways to do better next time, or stay away from that person.

What to Do With Negative Feedback

The biggest room in the world is the room for improvement. Try as you might, you will receive feedback on potential development areas. This is just part of life and applies to junior and senior practitioners alike.

Instead of seeing this as a negative thing, consider all feedback to be constructive. You can always learn something, if only to stay away from a certain person. More specifically, you will want to own the situation either way. Even if you do not agree with the feedback, don't argue with the feedback provider. Instead, show respect, and thank the person for the time taken to provide his or her opinion.

However, when the feedback is a game changer (e.g., something that clearly puts your reputation at risk), immediately get on the phone with or send an email to your mentor. Talk to your mentor about the feedback received, and share your own view. Your mentor will probably also share his or her opinion. Together, agree on how to best deal with the situation.

Note: Oftentimes, your mentor will informally reach out to the person that delivered the negative feedback to clarify and ensure that everything is settled before year-end ratings come around.

How to Deal With Good Feedback

When you receive positive feedback, don't get carried away. Keep working and leverage your newly recognized strengths. For your own development, and to cover yourself by supporting your mentor, always try to get good feedback in written form. If you received feedback via email or some digital feedback form, this can easily be forwarded to your mentor. No further action would be required.

In case of verbal feedback, however, you want to go a bit beyond the standard. Follow up with the feedback provider via email, thanking him or her for the discussion and stating the key points mentioned.

For example, in Project Bantiger, Daniela Lopez provided Adam with some intermittent feedback to help him in his professional development. Going forward, he should continue leveraging his analytical skills and focus on improving his client-interviewing skills. He sends the following note the same day:

Dear Daniela,

Thanks for your feedback earlier. I am glad you took the time to provide me with your view, as this will help me in my further development.

Being aware of both my strengths, such as analytical skills, and future development areas, namely client interviewing, will be very useful.

In case you have nothing to add, I will use this note as additional support for my year-end reference.

Thanks,
Adam

Usually, people do not come back at this point unless you fabricate something completely different from what has been discussed. Unless you hear back within a week, forward this email to your mentor as an FYI. Keep in mind, however, that this note should not replace a more formal written feedback from the project lead. This is just added on top – a bonus, if you will.

Key Takeaways

- Recognize the value of performance management. It ensures that effort is duly rewarded by identifying and eliminating poor performers. It also boosts your development by acknowledging your strengths and pointing you toward areas on which to focus.

- Know what to do and do it. Understand the performance management cycle and diligently perform your tasks throughout the year. This puts you in a good position for year-end ratings (provided you delivered high-quality work).

- Request feedback often. Feedback forms the basis for your performance rating, so don't leave anything to chance. Actively seek feedback for internal and external work and, ideally, get positive feedback in writing.

Part 3

Just Between Us

By now, we have discussed how to prepare yourself for your start in consulting and how to get things done on a daily basis. In the following section, I will shed some light on a variety of topics, ranging from managing your private life and preventing yourself from getting screwed by other practitioners to effectively pushing back when necessary and finding your sweet spot in the organization.

Irrespective of the firm you join, all of those topics will be part of your consulting life. Therefore, it is valuable to give this chapter a careful read and think about how these concepts directly apply to you.

CHAPTER 14
How to Manage Your Private Life

> "There's no such thing as work–life balance. There are work–life choices, and you make them, and they have consequences."
>
> **Jack Welch**

FAILING TO BALANCE WORK AND PRIVATE LIFE is what has driven many people before you to leave consulting. The point is, such a balance does not exist. Working in consulting is a lifestyle decision. Work may get in the way of social activities. People have tried to forge a balance before, but changing the system proved difficult.

The Reality

It's no secret that there is no such thing as a nine-to-five consulting job. You will work more than most of your colleagues from university who joined other industries. A brief discussion of overtime and taking vacation in consulting will make this very clear to you.

About Overtime

Depending on your firm, client base, and local regulations, you can expect to work anywhere between sixty and one hundred hours per week. That being said, the average will likely be at the lower end of this range. Don't buy in to the war stories from many people in the industry. More often than not, estimates of hours worked are wildly overestimated. I was not safe from this myself and realized that the actual hours worked are lower than you would believe in the heat of the moment.

However, even if you work only sixty hours, don't expect to work twelve hours straight from Monday to Friday. You will be working hours intermittently when everyone else is off, such as on weekends or late at night.

The reasons for having to work this much are manifold. As said before, you will be juggling both internal and external client requests simultaneously. These requests may be more or less urgent, and may be unanticipated.

While external client work is chargeable, internal work is not. For junior practitioners, this rarely makes a difference (although it sometimes can[22]). You will have to get all of your work done, regardless of whether it is chargeable or not.

Your firm might encourage you to work less, but most of the time, junior practitioners will work as long as necessary. (And let's not fool ourselves, it initially takes you longer, but your efficiency will improve with experience.) Usually, some daily rates will be charged to the client. Thus, it does not make a difference whether you work the planned eight hours or twenty, so long as you get the job done. This is clearly not the best situation to be in, because who really determines when the job is done? There is always something that can be improved or at least prepared for in advance.

Sometimes, project managers are instructed to work within a certain time budget and practitioners are told to charge all of the actual hours worked to the client. If you and your team suddenly end up working twenty hours per day for a week, which no engagement contract would ever project beforehand, your project manager will have to come up with a good explanation for your partner. However, before you get carried away, this is the exception to the rule. Don't count on being in such a luxurious situation, as more often than not, you'll be working for daily rates.

In short, you will work overtime, and you probably won't be compensated for doing so.

Vacation Is Key

With that in mind, you should obviously take holidays once in a while. Not only are you obligated to take some (if not all) during a given year, but your employer is probably encouraging you to take time off, too. (He is also obligated, and payouts are not the first choice.)

The trouble is, there might be a gap between official statements from your firm's leadership and actual practice on the ground. Quite simply, project work takes precedence. If you are on a project and would like to take a vacation, I would not set my hopes too high. The chance of being granted a break while on a project are very slim, unless:

- There is sudden downtime in the project itself.

- All key client personnel are unavailable.

- You have received approval to take vacation BEFORE starting the project.[23]

In other words, there is only one surefire way to take vacation: when you're not on a project. This can be done in two ways: proactively or reactively. The latter is common for most junior practitioners and basically means that you are taking time off when your project has finished and no other project is about to commence. Clearly, this is not ideal. Your travel plans will have to be rather spontaneous. Traveling by yourself will be easiest, but some people don't enjoy that.

Alternatively, you can try to lock in major parts of your annual vacation days in advance. If you have agreed upon and scheduled vacation days, your staffing manager will try to accommodate any future project requests. How to go about that is what we will look at in the final section of this chapter.

Communication With Your Loved Ones

It should not come as a surprise that your private life may suffer from your lack of time once you get up and running in your consulting job. I recommend you openly address this and tell your loved ones that you will

- have little time going forward,
- still want to meet them regularly, and therefore,
- have to become a bit more spontaneous (i.e., have to take advantage of any unexpected downtime).

I understand that this is not what many want to hear – and it is also not what corporate brochures use to attract high-caliber talent. This part probably sounds harsher than it actually is in reality, but if I learned one thing in consulting, it is that open, honest communication is the key to solving a lot of issues (and preventing most to begin with). Let's look at concrete steps that will enable you to make more of your available time.

How to Get the Most out of Your Time

If you look at your senior colleagues, most of them have learned over the years how to maximize their time. There are certain steps that can alleviate the pain. Consider adopting the following four techniques right away.

1. **Keep workdays free:** Workdays are for work only. This is not to say that you should forgo any pleasures if you can make time available. You should still take care of yourself.

   However, try to avoid blocking your evenings with commitments that are not work-related. When you are on a project and things heat up, a partner might be able to follow through with his (private) appointment, but you won't. Instead of always being the one cancelling at the last minute and slowly getting frustrated at yourself, save yourself from this situation to begin with and schedule your private activities involving other people on weekends only.

2. **Think of yourself first:** Ensure that you start every day on a high note. Do something that is meaningful to you just after waking up. This type of standard morning routine can lay the foundation for a happier and more productive day.

   Whether it is regular exercise, reading, doing yoga, or learning a language, do not schedule it for "sometime later in the day." That time will never come. It is far too easy to "call it a day" because you're exhausted at 2 a.m.

3. **Plan weekends ahead:** If you wait until you are absolutely certain that your project work is not going to interfere with your weekend, you will most likely not make the most of it.

For example, if you wait until Thursday afternoon to make plans for the weekend, chances are that you will not end up doing much – and end up spending your Sunday at the office. I know this because I have been there myself. Even if you don't have project work, there will always be a plausible reason (i.e., internal work) to go to the office on weekends.

Instead, do what the most successful and well-balanced practitioners do. At the beginning of the year, set aside some time with your partner (if applicable) to think about what you would like to do. If you want to get away for a weekend trip, decide on a specific weekend. Do this for as many weekends as you can and make preliminary arrangements (e.g., flights and accommodation).

If you do this, you will have a much greater likelihood of actually doing something worthwhile on your weekends. Even if there are busy weeks on your project, you'll figure it out just like prior to taking a vacation when you miraculously end up being the most productive. You will allocate your time accordingly (and if you finish your report while flying to your weekend getaway, then so be it).

4. **Plan vacations ahead:** What works for weekends applies to vacation as well. In fact, planning vacations well in advance is probably one of the things I should have learned much earlier myself. Once you have accumulated multiple weeks of vacation days, it will not get any easier to take them.

To actually make this happen, you should start early in the year. Set aside some time to go on vacation. Aim to have at least one full two-week vacation during the year. This will allow you to fully recharge your batteries and go back to work fresh. For specific steps to get your vacation requests approved, see Chapter 15.

Key Takeaways

- Accept that there is no work–life balance in consulting. Due to the dynamic nature of the industry, work will often interfere with private arrangements.

- Be realistic with respect to overtime. Most consultants at all levels work overtime, including weekends, but the majority of "war stories" tend to be exaggerated.

- Take your annual vacation. Up-front planning and early scheduling will increase the likelihood of going on holidays when it suits you, rather than when it suits your boss.

- Ask your family and friends for more spontaneity. You are going to have little time during the week, but effectively using unexpected downtime goes a long way to protecting and maintaining your social life.

- Separate work and private life. Block weekdays for work and plan weekends and vacation time in advance.

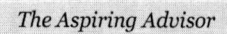

CHAPTER 15
How to Cover Your Ass

> "At the end of the day, man, you can't protect yourself from a haymaker that's coming in toward your face if you don't see it coming."
>
> **Busta Rhymes**

So far, we have covered several topics that form part of the core consulting skill set. The truth of the matter is, however, that none of this is going to save you every time. There are some situations that require street smarts, but navigating through these unusual situations does not have to be a daunting exercise.

People may try to screw you, both in consulting and elsewhere. Examples of this could easily fill an entire book. For now, let's clarify why you need to become good at covering yourself and illustrate this point using real-life examples.

Why You Need to Cover Yourself

Clearly, you should primarily be judged based on the work that you deliver. Unfortunately, that's not the case in the world we live in. When things turn ugly, people often try to cover themselves first.

Early in your career, you are at a significant disadvantage to more experienced colleagues. Unless someone tells you how things work, you will inevitably make mistakes at least once. However, there is no reason to make the same mistake that someone else has made if you can tap into that knowledge and experience.

In consulting, communication is everything. Given the fact that project-based work requires you to be "staffable," everyone should become his or her own marketer. You are essentially in a small marketplace offering your services. If your marketing does not work (i.e., you are largely unknown or have a poor reputation), then you have a problem. No project = no future.

Thus, you need to become adept at influencing communication to make your case, particularly when something goes wrong. Your mentor should be your primary guide in this, but it helps to be on top of this yourself. Remember, you are at the bottom of the corporate food chain. Therefore, the key is to address the root cause of potential issues and learn to take preventive measures.

For illustration purposes, we will use four scenarios that you will likely experience. These are project screwups, managing multiple expectations, vacations requests, and sudden project roll-offs. Use these examples as a reference, and try to adapt the underlying concepts to your specific case.

Example I: Project Screwup

Sooner or later, there will be problems in one of your projects. Sometimes, these are just minor hiccups that can be resolved easily. In rare cases, however, the problems can be more substantial. As a result, you may be reprimanded by your project manager for screwing up. If you really were responsible, then there is not much you can do but be humble, apologize, and try to perform better next time.

However, it may also happen that you had no involvement in the issue caused or even raised your concerns beforehand.[24] At face value, it makes sense to think that this should cover you, but it won't.

Your project manager has more clout in organizational dynamics, so you should expect him or her to use it if it helps avoid negative consequences for his or her upcoming promotion (not yours!). Your manager has experience and a network that may be leveraged at will in his or her favor. Thus, you would be the first one held accountable for issues you have not caused yourself in order to protect your manager's reputation. There are only two ways to mitigate such situations.

1. **Have written proof:** You will have to cover yourself before things turn ugly. Therefore, always ensure that you have written proof of what was discussed and what you might have disagreed with. If you can show that your project manager actually instructed you to go down a certain route that ultimately led to disaster, that's a good thing.

2. **Own the communication:** With your internal mentor, you should agree on one story that both of you will communicate. Obviously, this should be based on truth (at least the way you and your mentor perceive it). Whenever people ask you or your mentor what happened, you can utilize the exact same wording. Consistency and leaving little room for speculation are both essential.

To be sure, none of this is a guarantee that you will not suffer temporarily from a project screwup. You might, but the above steps will certainly increase the odds of coming out of the situation without long-term consequences.

Example II: Managing Multiple Expectations

Client projects should take precedence over internal work. That is true in theory, at least. In your day-to-day work, however, you will have to become good a juggling different tasks and responsibilities at the same time. Remember, you can't just drop internal work once a project kicks off.

Regardless of what these tasks may be, chances are good that you will run into capacity constraints at some point. I learned very quickly that junior consultants are not in a position to resolve such situations themselves other than by working extra hours.

However, what can you do when you might not be able to realistically produce different types of deliverables in time? Who should get priority, and why?

You will have to manage several stakeholders requesting your support. Do not choose sides: remain neutral. You do not know the *true* relationship between people and choosing sides can often backfire. Instead, play the "I'm inexperienced, please show me how" card. Put the ball back into your seniors' courts and let them figure it out. This is one of the few occasions when it is a wise move to sell yourself short.

Taking our Project Bantiger as an example, let's assume that Adam receives a request from Henk de Groot, his practice lead, to offer support on a proposal. Even though Adam has no availability before the upcoming PTI Steering Committee meeting, he knows that he cannot simply decline his boss's request. Responding directly to the request from Henk, Adam asks for guidance from Henk and Daniela, his current project manager, using the following format:

Dear Henk and Daniela,

My current capacity is rather stretched. I am therefore kindly asking for your guidance on how to proceed best.

As part of my role on Project Bantiger, I am currently working toward delivering the documents for the upcoming Steering Committee meeting by August 20, 2015. Meeting this deadline requires my full attention.

At the same time, I have been asked to provide some proposal support by August 19, 2015.

Right now, I cannot realistically guarantee the timely delivery of both with the quality you would expect.

Please advise on how to serve both of you best. If additional resources can support, I will be happy to provide any assistance necessary.

Thanks a lot for your guidance,

Adam

Adam might still end up working on both requests, which is exactly where he started. Chances are, however, that Henk and Daniela can alleviate some of the pressure by finding additional internal resources to support the proposal work.

Example III: Vacation Requests

We all need our breaks, and depending on labor regulations, your employer will be required to ensure that employees enjoy a minimum amount of holidays during any given year. Therefore, in principle, taking a vacation should be straightforward, and most people rarely experience any problems.

The trouble is, there are situations that will require you to change your plans. Unexpected project extensions or a sudden project start can put previously approved vacation time at risk. Moreover, you would not be the first one whose boss "does not recall" having approved your holidays. You need to decide on a case-by-case basis how flexible you want to be at that point.

To prevent you from having to continuously cancel your holidays on short notice, do what everyone else does with things that matter: get it in writing.

Requesting Vacation Approval

Ask your boss well in advance when you want to take vacation time. If you do this via email right away, you will want to make your request and then ask for a confirmation. For Adam on the Bantiger project, this would look as follows:

> *Dear Henk,*
>
> *As you are aware, I will be rolling off the Bantiger project on Friday, September 11, 2015.*
>
> *Unless you planned on my presence elsewhere, I would like to take this opportunity to go on vacation from September 14–25, 2015.*
>
> *Please let me know if this would work for you, so I can make the necessary travel arrangements.*
>
> *Many thanks,*
>
> *Adam*

Note: Adam should schedule a follow-up for one week later, as his vacation request is unlikely to be treated as a top priority.

Confirming Vacation Approval

More often than not, people request holidays in person or over the phone. In these cases, you will have to follow up via email immediately after. This will put you in an infinitely better position when your vacation is being put into question later on. Again, on Project Bantiger, this would look as follows:

Dear Henk,

Thanks a lot for taking the time earlier and approving my planned vacation. As discussed, I will be off from September 14–25, 2015.

Many thanks,

Adam

Example IV: Sudden Project Roll-Off

Finally, you might find yourself in a situation when you are unexpectedly told not to come to a project anymore. Also, rather than being informed in person or by phone, you might only receive a short text message from your project manager on a Sunday night.

If you cannot put your finger on why you were rolled off, what do you think other people will make of the situation? What impression does your sudden roll-off make? Exactly. Something smells fishy. Clearly, there must be a good reason why you are no longer supporting the engagement – even if there may not be one. Complaining about fairness won't do any good in such a case. You want to make every effort to avoid having anything hamper your reputation going forward.

Therefore, it is crucial to control the communication. This is difficult to accomplish but not impossible. You will have to align with

The Aspiring Advisor

some key people and get your version of the story out there. This is how I suggest you proceed (see Figure 12: Sudden Project Roll-Off Management).

1. **Mentor:** Call your mentor immediately after being suddenly taken off a project. Explain your view of the situation, listen to his or her guidance and settle on a coordinated approach.

2. **Boss:** Call your boss or send a text informing him or her of the changed situation. Don't worry if you have already received some form of negative feedback. Don't speculate, but tell him or her that you are still in the process of investigating. Mention your project manager's name and assure your boss that you will contact your staffing manager immediately.

3. **Staffing manager:** Call or meet your staffing manager in person. Tell him or her about the situation and identify potential staffing options.

4. **Other colleagues:** Eventually, colleagues will ask why you were suddenly rolled off your project. Tell them the story that you and your mentor agreed to put forward (which should be the truth).

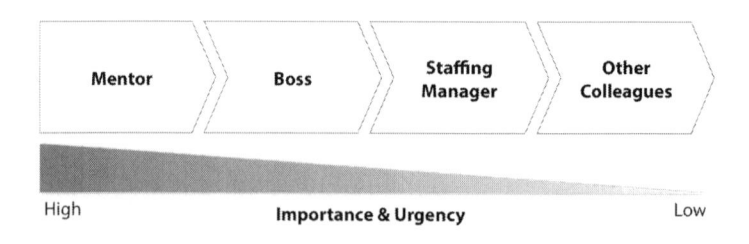

Figure 12: Sudden Project Roll-Off Management

Key Takeaways

- Expect unfair treatment at times. Learn to be street smart when you cover yourself, as core consulting skills will likely prove inadequate.

- Beware of project screwups. Project managers usually take responsibility but also understand that you are at a significant disadvantage unless you can back up your case with written correspondence and jointly steer internal communication with your mentor.

- Don't try to solve everything. When work requests collide, step back and ask for guidance from those senior people seeking your support. Attempting to prioritize by yourself will likely backfire.

- Get vacation requests confirmed in writing. Otherwise, you will always run the risk of having your plans cancelled on short notice.

- Carefully manage sudden project roll-offs. They pose a significant risk to your internal reputation. Try to quickly get a handle on internal communication.

CHAPTER 16

Saying No Without Ruining Your Career

> "I am only one, but still I am one. I cannot do everything, but still I can do something; and because I cannot do everything, I will not refuse to do something that I can do."
>
> **Edward Everett Hale**

I F YOU GET THE JOB DONE when others won't, you will be popular among your seniors. That is certainly a good thing, but there will be a point when you have to stop taking on further job assignments in order to avoid compromising the quality of your work.

In this chapter, we will look at how to handle such situations. I will share my take on why it's important to push back at times, and most importantly, show you how to do it.

Why Saying No Is Important

It is crucial to be selective when you provide support. If you never decline requests coming your way, you will soon experience a work overload that even the best consultants are unable to cope with. Let me be clear: This is not something you should consider within your first three months. At the start, pushing back should not be your concern.

You will soon notice that some people are more skilled at declining requests than others. Some simply seem to get by without much effort. At each level of the firm, you will meet different people broadly falling into one of four categories: misfits, dreamers, slaves, and drivers. These are distinct groups based on performance and pushback capabilities (Figure 13: Pushback vs. Performance Categories).

1. **Misfits** joined the firm with inaccurate expectations. They are often not very proactive, lack the right skills, or have realized that consulting was not for them. This shows in both their performance and willingness to push back. Their perceived indifference causes them to not last very long.

Figure 13: Pushback vs. Performance Categories

2. **Dreamers** hope to advance their career quickly. This is a good start, but ambition needs to be underpinned by quality work. How often have you met people who thought they were great assets while being average at best? They tend to be strategic in who and what they support (think visibility) using their pushback capabilities. The trouble is, there must be more to the pushback than just noise. Often, there is not. Thus, do not try to learn from this group.

3. **Slaves** are ambitious and are generally known as nice guys. None of this is bad, but understand that some senior people may exploit this because slaves are easy targets, and they usually get the job done.

4. **Drivers** tend to rise quickly in the firm by combining quality work with a reasonable degree of pushback (the main difference between them and "slaves"), and this is the key to a successful career. Drivers know where they are heading, what they are worth, and do not sell out to other people indefinitely, unless they see a way to also gain from it.

Again, focus on delivering great work at first, but over time, sharpen your skills in managing and declining tasks. If you never push back, especially when you are under pressure and there is little to gain from a given task, then you are making a mistake. You have to be somewhat selective, even picky, and develop a reputation for being difficult at times. However, don't come across as difficult just for the sake of it. It helps if you align closely with your boss or someone else you respect. People should know that you are working for _____ (name of person) and think twice before bothering you with their errands.

Should *You* Push Back?

To become a driver in declining requests, consider carefully whether you really want to push back. To help you make this decision, think through the following questions when a request comes your way:

- Do you have time to work on this request?

- Who is requesting your help? How important is this person in regard to:
    - Your performance rating at year-end
    - Future project opportunities
    - Other internal support (past or future)

- What is the request about? Is it generally in line with your interests or area of expertise?

- Does the request provide any other learning experience or some exposure (to the firm or senior leaders)?

Keep those questions in mind. This will become second nature very soon, as you will have a clear idea concerning with whom you want to and should be working.

There will be requests that you will probably deem unacceptable, but make no mistake, you can shine in each and every situation. For example, organizing catering for a meeting or taking care of late-night printing jobs can be great opportunities to showcase your reliability. (*Note*: Helping secure your boss's tourist visa for his or her upcoming holiday or picking up your boss' dry cleaning do not fall into this category.) That being said, don't simply decide that certain requests fall below your standard.

How to Push Back

So how do you push back without putting your career prospects on the line? Clearly, there is no one-size-fits-all solution here, but there are certain considerations that you should make when facing such a situation.

To begin with, there is a difference if someone meets you in person to ask for your help, rather than contacting you via email. The latter is preferred, as you can carefully consider your options, whereas you might be caught off guard when being approached directly.

However, turning down requests is best when done in person or by phone. Why? Because you don't want this outcome to stick around indefinitely and you don't want to leave traces. If, for some reason, you cannot push back in person or by phone, do so by writing a carefully crafted email in which you:

- Express gratitude for being considered for the job
- Show interest and motivation to support on that very subject (if applicable)
- State a specific reason for not being able to support this time
- Offer potential solutions (only if these are relevant, and make sure not to suggest fellow colleagues unless they have asked you to)
- Confirm your continued support

When You Do Not Have the Capacity

At times, you might not be able to support a project due to other work priorities. In such a case, you will have to decline the request in order to cover yourself. No one benefits from jobs done poorly due to being stretched too thin.

Therefore, simply respond by saying:

> *I would be happy to help, but due to severe capacity constraints, I may not be able to provide the support in the quality you rightly expect.*

The more specific you can be, the better. If you are already supporting some other senior colleague, mention his or her name. This is infinitely more powerful than just saying you had no time.

If all of this does not help, consider escalating the issue. Ideally, this would require a quick chat with whomever you are primarily working for, but at times, even that won't be enough. Let's look at this in sequence.

1. **Let the big guys handle it:** Call your boss (or whoever you are working for) to have him or her provide guidance on the issue. State your concerns and ask him or her what the next steps should be. More often than not, you will get a response along the lines of "Leave it to me . . . ," in which case your boss will solve the issue for you.

   If you are given other instructions, get back to the original requestor by email, remembering to cc your boss and decline once.

   For example, in Project Bantiger, Adam was asked by some other senior colleague to support on some internal work. Since he did not have the capacity, Adam agreed with Henk de Groot, his boss, to turn down the request. He opened his response by writing:

   As discussed with Henk de Groot, . . .

2. **Take matters into your own hands (only when you have to):** If you cannot get in touch with your boss, or if you are in the middle of something urgent that cannot wait while the second requester is pushing you hard, try to resolve the matter on your own. It goes without saying that this is not recommended, but consider it to be an exception. If you still want to go ahead, it is important to be brief and specific in your communication.

   Write a short email to both your boss and the requestor that a) asks them to provide guidance on how to proceed best or b) informs them that you cannot satisfy the request at this stage due to the very assignment at hand. A possible script can be found in Chapter 15.

   Once sent out, get back to your work. Don't engage in follow-up communication until you have accomplished the task you mentioned as your current priority.

To be sure, escalation should not be your default reaction. Keep in mind that some people might be put off by such bold moves. Nevertheless, recognize that there are situations that you will not be able to manage on your own, regardless of what you may think, who you know, or what you have accomplished in the past.

At one point or another, I have made all the mistakes that I am now encouraging you not to make. For example, due to an enormous project ramp-up phase, some internal work was unlikely to be finished within a given timeframe. In anticipation of this, I reached out to the person in charge of the internal work to explain that I would not be able to continue to support on the project. I thought this was not only the right thing to do, but I even felt proud of being proactive and raising issues up front. Unfortunately, this did not go over well with the senior person on the other end. What then commenced was what we call "email ping-pong." Known for having a strong hierarchical mindset, this person bombarded me with emails seemingly every minute. Same message, different wording.

Essentially, my concerns were deemed irrelevant and I was expected to deliver regardless. In the heat of the moment, I simply responded that I had no time to discuss this any further and was sure that our staffing manager would be willing to find someone with available capacity. (Don't do this!)

The story did not end there. By the following morning, I had received a meeting invitation from that senior person concerning "Ways of Working and Expectations." Mind you, I was well into my second year. I stood my ground, but going forward, this person proved to be a pain when it came to performance ratings and other aspects of my progress.

To put it simply, think twice before trying to solve things on your own. Your actions will most likely backfire. Even so, taking a stand every once in a while will probably not hurt too much.

When You Are Just Not Interested

At other times, you might have a lull in your work (*read*: you could somehow squeeze this additional task in), but you still don't want to be in charge of a certain task. In such cases, you cannot simply make up additional work as an excuse.

Instead, you have to apply tactics that I learned from a fellow junior colleague on my first project. After having carefully considered the request, you might come to the conclusion that there is simply not much in it for you. Neither the person asking for help, nor the request itself, brings meaningful benefits. In such cases, take the leap to become a driver and respond by:

- Saying that you are happy to help

- Mentioning any upcoming priorities (to set the right expectation that this might not be an ongoing relationship). For example, in Adam's case with Project Bantiger, he could write the following:

Please note that I will be on Project Bantiger with Daniela Lopez from August 3, 2015...

- Requesting feedback upon completion of the job (rule of thumb: whenever you work for more than twenty hours on a job)

To help me in my further development and for upcoming year-end discussions, I would kindly ask you for some short written feedback upon completion of the task.

This is crucial. Few people will be overly enthusiastic about writing yet more feedback, and as a result, the original request will often land on someone else's desk.

Key Takeaways

- Learn to turn down requests. Pushing back is a vital skill to enable you to focus on delivering great work when your capacity is already stretched.

- Copy those who have mastered the art of pushback to avoid being exploited. These drivers stand out from misfits, dreamers, and slaves in terms of performance and pushback capabilities.

- Don't be too selective when accepting work requests at the beginning of your career. Regard everything as a learning opportunity, but be mindful if you cannot continue to deliver a superior quality of work.

- Don't overtly push back. Instead, turn to your senior colleagues for guidance and potential mediation.

- Tactically ask for feedback in return for your support when you are not interested in a certain job. Almost magically, those work requests will disappear.

CHAPTER 17
Stop Thinking and Execute

> "It was the Law of the Sea, they said. Civilization ends at the waterline. Beyond that, we all enter the food chain, and not always right at the top."
>
> **Hunter S. Thompson,**
> ***Generation of Swine: Tales of Shame and Degradation in the '80s***

CONSULTING IS ONE OF THE BEST PROFESSIONS, at least at an early point in your career (see the Appendix for my take on why people should start a career in consulting), but all that glitters is not gold. Most people will not tell you how you will be treated as a junior and what this actually means for your life.

Make no mistake, perception becomes reality. Whether you agree or not, the way others perceive you directly impacts your standing in the organization and the opportunities you're offered. We have discussed the perception of junior practitioners throughout this book. Chapters 2, 3, 4, and 11 have tackled this subject from different angles.

Now, let me offer a more personal take on this process of preparing you for the ultimate cause of frustration: the constant requests to do less than you feel capable of doing. At the end of this chapter, you will know exactly what you're getting yourself into and how to best cope with it.

You Don't Know Much

As a junior consultant, you will notice sooner or later that no one cares much about your past accomplishments. Your educational accolades are irrelevant. Where you graduated from might have helped you to get the job, but going forward it will matter very little.

By and large, you are supposed to follow instructions and focus on execution. The actual thinking will be taken care of by more experienced colleagues, as you may not be qualified to do so. Whether you like it or not, you will have to earn trust before people start listening to you. You can safely keep your ideas and concerns to yourself for now. You will rarely benefit in any professional way from speaking up this early in the game.

Obviously, few would ever put it quite like that, but based on my experience and research on the ground, I am confident that this is the impression a lot of junior practitioners get.

Nobody Said It Was Going to Be Fair

If you're lucky, then you're working for someone you can look up to – someone who you fully respect for his or her wisdom, expertise, principles, or experience. That is not going to be the case all the time. In fact, there are more than a few leaders who are far from great.[25]

Now, imagine that you're working hard without receiving any recognition for an extended period of time. What will happen? Obviously, it will have a negative impact on your motivation. You will begin to ask yourself why you should keep up the effort and work all those hours, especially when you don't really feel like doing it.

Don't let this deter you. If you buy into the expectation of focusing only on execution, then your creativity will falter. It is as if your brain slowly falls apart due to insufficient exercise. Over time, you stop having ideas, both good and bad. Don't let this happen. Instead, use your mental brain capacity elsewhere.

Don't Let Your Mental Capacity Deteriorate

If you have read Chapter 10 on continuous learning, then the following information will sound familiar. I refer to it again because I believe it's critical.

For starters, I encourage you to speak up if you truly feel that you need to. You will likely have to pay a price for doing so, but you will feel better, and, chances are, someone will recognize you and provide invaluable career support. Then again, this will not come without risks. You might end up not lasting very long in the firm, but ultimately, this is your choice.

If you do not want to risk it and prefer to keep a low profile, at least adopt the two habits already presented in Chapter 10 which are reviewed below:

- Reading every day

- Writing down new ideas every day

Both habits, if successfully adopted, will ensure that you keep using your idea muscle.

When Your Boss Is Really Bad . . .

Finally, let's shed some light on what to do when you're working for a bad boss – or any other senior colleague, for that matter. When I say "bad," I mean "really bad." Personality or character traits aside, we are referring to skills here. So, what do you do if you have a boss, or other senior-level practitioner working with you, that you consider completely incompetent? We have all been there at some point. If you have not, trust me, you'll have the experience eventually.

Unless you want to leave the firm, taking the following principles into account is likely the wisest thing you can do.

- **Continue delivering good work:** No matter how much you suffer, nothing justifies doing a poor job. You have to serve the business first, regardless of whether your boss is competent or not. In fact, if your work helps to advance your boss's career, so be it.

- **Learn from your boss:** Don't waste your time thinking about how bad your boss is, as it won't solve the problem. In fact, he or she probably has some sort of skill set that allowed him or her to be promoted this far. Try to figure out what your boss does well – maybe better than anyone else.

- **Speak to your mentor:** Seek out your mentor for guidance. Chances are, your mentor knows more about your boss' background than you do. Your mentor may also advise you on how to best proceed.

- **Stay close to people you admire:** Identify those colleagues that you really look up to. If they are in your team, working together more closely should be simple. If they are not in your team, get in touch with them anyway, and try to provide them with support on some internal projects with which they are dealing. Everyone is happy to receive additional support, and this might be the first step in a long and successful professional relationship.

For more information on how to navigate the consulting stakeholder landscape, reread Chapters 4 and 11.

Key Takeaways

- Forget previous accolades and accomplishments. They are largely irrelevant. Expect many senior practitioners to ask juniors to focus on executing what they have dreamed up.

- Never get discouraged. Work on yourself and keep your mind active through regular reading and seeking to become an idea machine.

- Learn from each experience. Over time, carve out your sweet spot in the organization by identifying and staying close to people whose values you share. Remember that you cannot change the system.

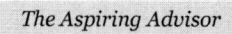

Part 4

Leaving the Firm

A JUNIOR CONSULTANT'S LIFE CYCLE would not be complete if it did not include a potential end of one's consulting career. This is what we will focus on in the subsequent pages. Let's acknowledge that not everyone is meant to work in consulting all their lives. Chapter 18 provides a decision-making framework when you first start thinking about jumping ship. Chapter 19 explicitly lays out what should be done – and why – in case one decides to leave.

CHAPTER 18
Should You Leave the Firm?

> "Would you tell me, please, which way I ought to go from here?"
> "That depends a good deal on where you want to get to," said the Cat.
> "I don't much care where –" said Alice.
> "Then it doesn't matter which way you go," said the Cat.
>
> **Lewis Carroll,**
> ***Alice's Adventures in Wonderland***

EVEN THE BEST WORKING ENVIRONMENT TURNS SOUR sometimes and you might start thinking about whether to move on. You will ask yourself if consulting is really for you. You will start questioning whether you would benefit from starting fresh in another firm. You will ponder whether to seek out new opportunities by perhaps joining a client company.

This chapter will not give you the answers to these questions, but it will provide you with a structured decision-making framework once your initial questioning has become more material. The steps I offer are simple and straightforward. As such, they can be applied without much difficulty, and do not complicate things more than they have to be.

Going Back to Where It All Started

Before spending too much time thinking about whether to change careers or not, you should look at your current situation from a different angle. Instead of weighing the pros and cons of making a change, first consider where you have come from. Think about what originally got you into consulting. (If you have done the personal pitch in Chapter 2 then review your answers to Questions 6 and 7 about your expectations.)

The decision tree (Figure 14: Career Change Decision Tree) will guide you in determining whether or not a change is truly necessary, and, if so, what that change may be. It is crucially important, however, to work through this exercise with full honesty. Otherwise, the exercise is essentially pointless.

Thinking It Through

If you have found that your current work is not in line with your core motivation or original expectations, you should consider alternative options. To do this systematically, answer the following questions.

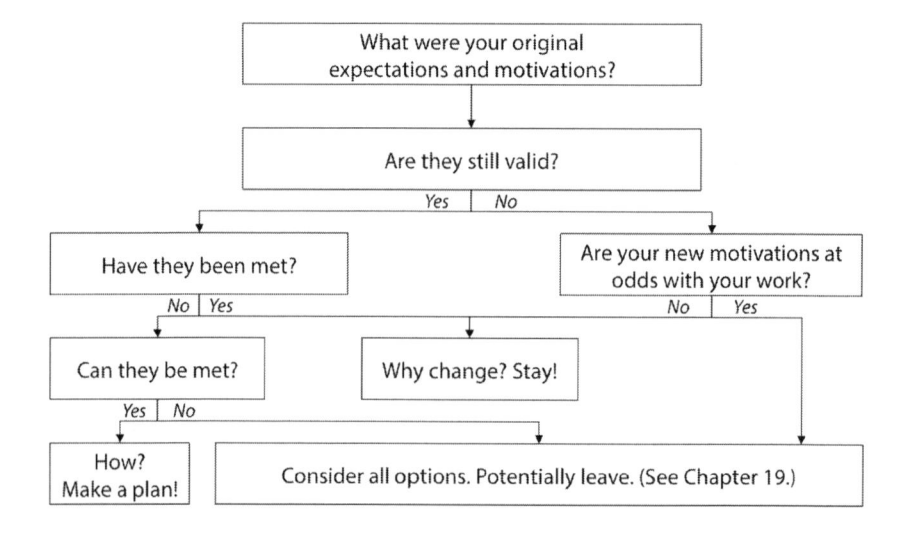

Figure 14: Career Change Decision Tree

1. **What is your ultimate objective?** Think about what you want to accomplish. Clarify what success would mean to you. Most likely, you will come up with a handful of different aspects that are important to you. Since they are hardly equal in importance, go ahead and prioritize them.

2. **What are your options?** List all the options you have when leaving your job. Be realistic, but don't limit your imagination too much. Transferring to another department or internationally? Joining a former client? Starting your own business? Traveling the world? Doing a PhD? There are countless options. It is completely up to you.

3. **What is there to gain from each option?** Be specific about the potential benefits from each option.

4. **What are the downsides of each option?** Most decisions require a trade-off. By opting for one, you will likely have to forgo something else. What aspect of each of your options do you consider less than ideal? In other words, what don't you like about the likely impact from choosing any one option?

5. **Which options can you eliminate right away?** Based on your assessment of both pros and cons, which options appear to be completely at odds with your ideal outcome? Reduce the number of options down to two or three at most.

6. **How could you mitigate remaining downsides?** When considering your final option(s), try to identify

ways to mitigate the negative aspects. This will help you identify the best option and should help to include all of your desired objectives from Step 1.

7. **What is the next step?** Whatever your final decision, ensure that you follow through. Use the momentum gained from this exercise and decide on the next several next steps, if possible. Do at least one thing today, and schedule the rest for the future. This increases the likelihood of actually moving closer to your goal.

Considering all this, what is your ultimate decision? It's crucial to spend some time on this choice and not rush ahead.

Key Takeaways

- Be open to new ventures. Career changes are common in all industries. Consulting is no different, albeit the dynamic work with changing projects may lend itself more to temporary frustrations than long-term unhappiness.

- Make career decisions systematically. Use a structured decision-making process to determine whether a career change is indeed necessary. Oftentimes, minor steps can be taken to avoid the process of changing firms or industries.

- Identify and evaluate all viable career change options. This process lays the groundwork for a more satisfying career track if your current consulting work is no longer meeting your objectives.

CHAPTER 19

If You Decide to Leave the Firm

> "The hardest thing to learn in life is which bridge to cross and which to burn."
>
> **David Russell**

THIS IS THE FINAL CHAPTER, and in a way, this will close the loop. This chapter assumes that you have decided to leave the firm, as discussed in Chapter 18. Against that background, we will now look at *how* you should leave.

Contrary to what many may say, burning bridges is the wrong thing to do. Leaving any work environment requires ticking boxes in two categories: professional and personal.

The professional category is all about your previously established work commitments and areas of responsibility. This is what we will discuss first. We will look at what you need to do in order to avoid having things fall apart once you are gone.

We will then focus on the personal category, which is about the relationships you have developed in your firm. We will discuss how to set up your relationships for the future within the process of saying good-bye.

Laying the Groundwork for Your Departure

Once you have decided to leave the firm, you will have to finalize your departure. The exact process may differ between firms, but by and large, to accomplish this you will want to:

- Arrange your departure with your boss and HR
- Clear the way for departure

Let us look at both steps in more detail.

Arranging Your Departure With Your Boss and HR

Making the decision to leave is not an easy one. Telling your boss, who has hired you, is even trickier. Even if your boss is one of the reasons for your resignation, you will likely feel uncomfortable bringing up the topic of leaving. Nevertheless, don't spend too much time waiting (and second-guessing) before you seek a final discussion with your boss. Find time in his or her agenda and prepare as you would for any other important conversation (e.g., a job interview).

When you meet your boss, be absolutely clear about what you want. Your decision should already be made. Now, it's just about agreeing on details, such as leaving dates, holiday payout, etc.

In addition, you should clearly understand and be able to explain the reasons why you're leaving and the exact wording thereof. Of course, you could tell your boss that he or she "sucks," but you can probably predict what that would mean for your reputation within the firm, as well as any future relationships with your colleagues. You will want to be authentic but also tactful. Therefore, inform your boss about your departure and:

- State that your decision is final

- Make it clear that this decision was not an easy one to make and you've thought it through

- Thank him or her for the trust and learning opportunities you have received from the firm

- Emphasize that this is not a decision against the firm or its people, but solely for personal reasons

- Mention a reason for your choice (e.g., change of environment, consulting is not for you, family)

- Confirm that all of your tasks and responsibilities will either be completed or officially handed over to others prior to your departure

- Ask to stay in contact with him or her even after you have left the firm

You would not be the first consultant to become completely disillusioned once you announce your exit to your boss. Chances are, you will be asked to keep a low profile and not tell other people about your move. Acknowledge your boss's concerns by stating that you respect his or her views and will work toward minimizing any disruptions as much as possible. This means that you will not engage in any badmouthing; instead, you will use the time available to nurture existing relationships.

You should also not be surprised when the relationship between you and your boss, as well as other members of the team, changes drastically from one day to the next. Some people tend to take it personally when a member of the team decides to go a different way. They feel mistreated and all trust is often lost. You can't do much about this. You need to understand that this might happen, but continue to maintain your professional attitude and follow your own path.

Apart from meeting your boss, you will have to align on administrative requirements with your HR department. They will usually provide you with a checklist of things to complete prior to leaving. This should be rather straightforward. Most likely, the talk with HR will be a breeze. They are used to having these discussions and will therefore not make it more difficult on you than necessary.

Clearing Your Way to Departure

One of things you should have mentioned to your boss is how to deal with ongoing tasks and responsibilities. You cannot simply drop everything once you have agreed to leave the firm. Most likely, your boss will have his or her own expectations of what needs to be finalized before your departure. Whether you are given a list of items to cross off or not, you should spend some of your own time identifying all the items that you are currently associated with in some form or other. To accomplish this, think through the following questions:

1. What tasks are you currently working on, either by yourself or as part of a team? What other tasks have you been assigned to? What roles do you perform?

2. What is the state of each of those tasks or roles?

3. What are the next steps for each of those tasks or roles?

4. Which of the upcoming steps can be accomplished personally, and by when can you complete them?

5. If any other next steps need to be completed or continued by someone else, who will have the capacity and will-

ingness to do so? Thus, whom can you hand these tasks over to?

Once you have worked through the above questions, come up with a concise plan of how to finalize all this. The function of this exercise is to cover yourself by preventing things from falling apart when you leave. You can (and should) proactively communicate this plan to your boss before your departure. This will give him or her further confidence in your professionalism and will minimize any potential negative sentiments toward you once you are gone.

You Always Meet Twice

Apart from terminating all your work commitments, let's look at the personal aspect of farewell management. You will want to make sure that the connections you have invested in over months or years are not lost once you leave the firm. There is a German idiom that literally translates to, "You always meet people twice in a lifetime." While the original meaning is more about doing unto others as you would have them do unto you, I believe in the idea of repeat encounters in a completely different context. With that in mind, it is crucial not only to build, but also to maintain your network when you make the choice to move on.

To accomplish this, do what works in any networking context: come up with a plan and focus on execution. I will show you what this translates to in consulting and how to do this in the remainder of this chapter.

5-Step Process to Leaving the Firm and Taking Relationships with You

In order to maintain your relationships, you will have to proceed strategically. This is best accomplished by following a tried-and-tested 5-step process.

1. **List key people:** For starters, come up with a list of all those people that you deem important. These might be colleagues with whom you are friends, colleagues you have learned something from, or simply people you like or sincerely respect. This list may be a long one. Don't limit your list to your peers, either; consider junior and senior practitioners alike.

2. **Meet key people individually:** Go through the list and identify key people you would like to meet with individually. Depending on agendas, you should agree to meet for coffee, lunch, dinner, or in any other nonwork environment to have some personal conversation. These occasions will serve as crucial moments to connect. You will be able to:

   – Express your gratitude for their support (or whatever applies)

   – Clarify your reasoning for leaving the firm directly to them

   – Speak about potential next steps

3. **Invite all people:** Invite all of the people you listed in Step 1 to a final round of farewell drinks. The invitation should be sent out as one message at least two weeks in advance. Whether the drinks are scheduled before or after your leave does not really matter. If you can afford it, pay for the drinks and snacks. Regard this occasion as an investment in your future.

4. **Make yourself findable online:** This is a no-brainer. Unless you have been living under a rock, you should have various social media profiles by this time. If not,

now is the time to set them up. Focus primarily on professional networks, e.g., LinkedIn or Xing.

5. **Stay connected:** Sift through the list of people and see if you are connected with them online. Ideally, you will want to have all of them as contacts in your professional network.

How About the Leaving Email?

Many people think about taking their network of relationships beyond their current employer. However, they only do this half-heartedly and usually at the last minute. Let's be clear: It is not enough to send a farewell email to "Corporate All" on the day of your departure. It is also useless to request ongoing contact by providing private contact details. Ninety-nine percent of the time, this email will not be followed up upon in any way.

You have to take matters into your own hands and connect proactively. Make the first step. Don't wait for others to connect with you.

Key Takeaways

- Don't burn bridges. Nurture key relationships and take them beyond your current employer when leaving the firm. Lay the foundation for ongoing relationships.

- Inform your boss about your intended departure first. Reiterate that your leaving will cause minimal disruptions to the business because you will finalize open items or conduct thorough handovers.

- Invest in your departure. Individual catch-ups (e.g., over lunch or coffee) and a common farewell event can serve as practical investments to leave on a positive note.

The Aspiring Advisor

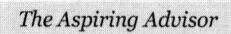

Final Thoughts

In the preface, I described the circumstances that made me launch this book project. I have tried to include all the insights my colleagues and I have gained to fill this need for a reference guide for junior consultants. As such, I hope these pages can contribute to the industry in at least in two ways.

First, I am confident that those just starting out will benefit from it. While no handbook can guarantee success, I believe that this book will put new joiners on a very solid platform from which to launch their careers. This does not mean that it may not be a bumpy road, as it most certainly will be. However, making mistakes is nothing to be worried about. It is a normal part of learning new things. However, making the same mistakes others have made before is just dumb. I believe this book enables junior practitioners to get on the fast track and stay there.

Second, I hope this book also benefits current senior practitioners. Instead of explaining what good performance means and – even worse – arguing why something should be done, this is a guide that can be handed out to those just starting out. Ideally, those joining the firm will already be better prepared than others in the past.

If you have read each chapter line by line, then you might still be wondering about the very first word of this book: *Teflon*. This goes back to one of the very first lessons I learned on the job. It is also one of the lessons that I cherish the most.

It must have been my second month with the firm. I was supporting an external client engagement with many different stakeholders and I was working closely with my project manager, who coordinated the entire piece of work. Due to increasing demands on a certain stakeholder, we agreed to provide additional ad hoc support to her. Upon offering my help in person, she launched into a ten-minute rant against various people on the team and held me, the most junior by far, accountable. Essentially, I was the recipient of pressure that must have been building up over months and was now finally being released.

Literally shaking, I left to report back to my project manager. He apparently knew that something like that was about to happen and immediately said, "Teflon, Moritz. Teflon." He then went on to explain the concept of the "Teflon suit." For various reasons, people sometimes lose it and resort to personal insults, both in business and private life. On such occasions, it helps to wear one's mental "Teflon suit," which helps maintain one's professional countenance. That's the story of Teflon.

Just as I benefited from all of the advice passed on to me, I hope this book will do the same for you. Please let me know how you have applied some of the concepts laid out in this book. Let me hear your story or feedback via Twitter at @MoritzDressel or at AspiringAdvisor.com. Till then, keep rocking and stay on the rise.

Appendix

In this part, I have included some additional information that you might find helpful. More specifically, you will find:

- Useful books
- Other useful resources

Useful Books

Below, I have listed a number of books that have either influenced me or my colleagues, or those we consider to be must-reads in any field.

Presentation Design

- Reynolds, Garr. *Presentation Zen: Simple Ideas on Presentation Design and Delivery.* Berkeley, CA: New Riders Pub., 2008.

- Duarte, Nancy. *Slide:ology: The Art and Science of Creating Great Presentations.* Beijing: O'Reilly Media, 2008.

Networking and Relationship Building

- Ferrazzi, Keith, and Tahl Raz. *Never Eat Alone: And Other Secrets to Success, One Relationship at a Time.* New York: Random House, 2005.

- Carnegie, Dale. *How to Win Friends and Influence People.* New York: Pocket Books, 1998.

- Cialdini, Robert B. *Influence: The Psychology of Persuasion.* New York: Collins, 2007.

Consulting Skills and Client Interaction

- Barney, Jay B., and Trish Gorman Clifford. *What I Didn't Learn in Business School: How Strategy Works in the Real World.* Boston: Harvard Business Review, 2010.

- Maister, David H., Charles H. Green, and Robert M. Galford. *The Trusted Advisor.* New York: Simon & Schuster, 2000.

- Mintzberg, Henry, Bruce W. Ahlstrand, and Joseph Lampel. *Strategy Safari.* Harlow, UK: FT Prentice Hall, 2009.

- Rasiel, Ethan M., and Paul N. Friga. *The McKinsey Mind: Understanding and Implementing the Problem-Solving Tools and Management Techniques of the World's Top Strategic Consulting Firm.* Chicago: McGraw-Hill, 2002.

Time Management

- Glei, Jocelyn K. *Manage Your Day-to-Day: Build Your Routine, Find Your Focus, and Sharpen Your Creative Mind.* Las Vegas: Amazon Publishing, 2013.

- Belsky, Scott. *Making Ideas Happen: Overcoming the Obstacles between Vision and Reality*. New York: Portfolio, 2010.

Career Building

- Newport, Cal. *So Good They Can't Ignore You: Why Skills Trump Passion in the Quest for Work You Love*. New York: Business Plus, 2012.

- Arden, Paul. *It's Not How Good You Are, It's How Good You Want to Be*. London: Phaidon, 2003.

- Peters, Thomas J. *The Brand You 50, or, Fifty Ways to Transform Yourself from an "Employee" into a Brand That Shouts Distinction, Commitment, and Passion!* New York: Knopf, 1999.

- Pfeffer, Jeffrey. *Power: Why Some People Have It – and Others Don't*. New York: Harper Business, 2010.

Communication, Writing, and Structured Thinking

- Heath, Chip, and Dan Heath. *Made to Stick: Why Some Ideas Survive and Others Die*. New York: Random House, 2007.

- Hertz, Noreena. *Eyes Wide Open: How to Make Smart Decisions in a Confusing World*. London: William Collins, 2013.

- Minto, Barbara. *The Pyramid Principle: Logic in Writing and Thinking*. London: Financial Times Prentice Hall, 2002.

- Weiner, Allen. *So Smart But . . . : How Intelligent People Lose Credibility – and How They Can Get It Back*. San Francisco: Jossey-Bass, 2007.

Other Useful Resources

Below, I have also provided a number of additional items I deem useful for those starting out in consulting. I don't expect everyone to benefit from them equally, but I believe that they will be a great help for some in their day-to-day working lives.

Online Tools and Applications

- Wunderlist: Task management application (see Chapter 9 for additional information).

- Nextcall: Application (Android only) that tracks the last time you have called any of your contacts, allows you to set how often you want to stay in touch, and reminds you accordingly.

- Text expansion apps: Using predefined text snippets via shortcuts saves time for recurring writing tasks. The recommended options are PhraseExpress (for Windows) and TextExpander (for Mac).

- Clipboard manager: Do not limit yourself to one item in your clipboard. Use a clipboard manager instead, such as Ditto Clipboard Manager, ClipX, or ArsClip (all free).

- Outlook add-ons: Equip your corporate mailbox with missing functionalities using Live Inbox (USD 30), OutlookFinder (free), or Lookeen (free).

- Every Time Zone: Find time zones and corresponding times in one view (www.everytimezone.com).

Excel Modeling Resources

Online

- MrExcel Forum (www.mrexcel.com/forum/index.php)
- Stackoverflow Excel and VBA section (www.stackoverflow.com/questions/tagged/excel-vba?sort=newest)
- VBA Express Forum (www.vbaexpress.com/forum/forum.php)

Books

- Bendoly, Elliot. *Excel Basics to Blackbelt: An Accelerated Guide to Decision Support Designs.* Cambridge: Cambridge UP, 2008.
- Jelen, Bill, and Michael Alexander. *Excel 2013 Pivot Table Data Crunching.* New York: Pearson Education, 2013.

Lifestyle Enhancement

- Scientific Seven: A full-body workout that takes only seven minutes to complete and requires nothing but your bodyweight (*read:* can be done in hotel rooms)

Notes

1. The project name "Bantiger" is a reference to a mountain where Consulting Inc. and PTI signed the project agreement (engagement letter).

2. Some seniors may delegate because they actually seek novel input from you. Whether they are the majority is a different story.

3. For a detailed breakdown of the reasons for starting a consulting career, visit: www.moritzdressel.com/start-your-career-in-consulting.html

4. Godin, Seth. "Do You Have the Right to Be Heard?" http://sethgodin.typepad.com/seths_blog/. June 26, 2010. Accessed May 24, 2015.

5. Be somewhat mindful about what you truly want to share. At the end of the day, it is all about trust, and trust can be exploited. If you are very open, you might get hurt. If you don't share your views, you might feel miserable. Choose the path that suits you best. I opted for the former and have not regretted it.

6 It is good practice to create a new Outlook Data File (.pst) for each project. The entire communication stream can then easily be saved in a shared drive after project completion.

7 This is not exclusive to consulting. If you are willing to pay the price, and reap the benefits, then make this your *modus operandi*.

8 The Radicati Group, *Email Statistics Report 2011–2015*. Palo Alto, CA, 2015.

9 Chui, Michael. *The Social Economy Unlocking Value and Productivity through Social Technologies*. New York: McKinsey & Company, 2013.

10 This is independent of company size. There are Fortune 500 firms where any attachment larger than 10 MB will be blocked.

11 Whenever you use USB keys for work purposes, make sure they are encrypted.

12 Danziger, Shai, Jonathan Levav, and Liora Avnaim-Pesso. "Extraneous Factors in Judicial Decisions." *Proceedings of the National Academy of Sciences*, 2011, 6889–92.

13 https://www.wunderlist.com

14 It is common for practitioners to request that the project sponsor officially announce the arrival of external advisors, reiterate the importance of the objective as well as the initiative, and call on members of the organization to make themselves available. Without such communication, most projects relying on internal support are doomed to fail.

15 Ericsson, Karl Anders. *The Road to Excellence: The Acquisition of Expert Performance in the Arts and Sciences, Sports, and Games*. Mahwah, N. J.: Lawrence Erlbaum Associates, 1996.

16 Ferriss, Timothy. *The 4-Hour Workweek: Escape 9–5, Live Anywhere, and Join the New Rich*. New York: Crown Publishers, 2007.

17 Johnson, Steven. *Where Good Ideas Come From: The Natural History of Innovation*. New York: Riverhead Books, 2010.

18 Altucher, James. "The Ultimate Guide for Becoming an Idea Machine." Altucher Confidential. 2014. Accessed May 24, 2015.

19 Altucher, Claudia Azula, and James Altucher. *Become an Idea Machine: Because Ideas Are the Currency of the 21st Century*. CreateSpace Independent Publishing, 2014.

20 SMART is an abbreviation for objectives or goals that are *S*pecific, *M*easurable, *A*chievable, *R*elevant, and *T*ime-Bound.

21 Pfeffer, Jeffrey. *Power: Why Some People Have It – and Others Don't*. New York: Harper Business, 2010.

22 Some firms measure performance primarily based on "utilization," which is the ratio of total client hours billed versus the total hours in a year. Hence, the higher the number of hours worked for external clients, the higher your chances for a good performance rating.

23 Sure enough, this is no guarantee you will actually end up taking your holidays. There will be situations in which you may be asked to cancel your arrangements.

24 It is recommended that you never start a project without setting up a risk and issue tracker. Take the initiative in case your manager does not request this.

25 Goleman, Daniel, and Richard E. Boyatzis. *Primal Leadership: Unleashing the Power of Emotional Intelligence*. Tenth Anniversary ed., Boston: Harvard Business Review Press, 2013.

Printed in Great Britain
by Amazon